ETHNIC STUDIES and MULTICULTURALISM

SUNY Series
FRONTIERS IN EDUCATION
Philip G. Altbach, editor

The Frontiers in Education Series draws upon a range of disciplines and approaches in the analysis of contemporary educational issues and concerns. Books in the series help to reinterpret established fields of scholarship in education by encouraging the latest synthesis and research. A special focus highlights educational policy issues from a multidisciplinary perspective. The series is published in cooperation with the School of Education, Boston College. A complete listing of the books in this series can be found at the end of this volume.

ETHNIC STUDIES and MULTICULTURALISM

THOMAS J. LA BELLE
and CHRISTOPHER R. WARD

State University of New York Press

Published by
State University of New York Press

For information, address the State University of New York Press,
State University Plaza, Albany, NY 12246

Production by Christine Lynch
Marketing by Dana E. Yanulavich

Library of Congress Cataloging-in-Publication Data

La Belle, Thomas J.
    Ethnic Studies and multiculturalism / Thomas J. La Belle and
Christopher R. Ward.
        p.   cm. — (SUNY series, frontiers in education)
    Includes bibliographical references and index.
    ISBN 0-7914-2984-9 (PB : acid free). — ISBN 0 -7914-2983-0 (CH :
acid free)
    1. Ethnology—Study and teaching (Higher)—United States.
2. Multicultural education—United States.   3. Pluralism (Social
sciences)—Study and teaching (Higher)—United States.   4. United
States—Race relations—Study and teaching (Higher) 5. United
States—Ethnic relations—Study and teaching (Higher)   I. Ward,
Christopher R., 1948–   . II. Title. III. Series.
E184.A1B35   1996
305.8'0071'173—dc20   95-73748
                                                          CIP

10 9 8 7 6 5 4 3 2 1

Dedicated to former students Robert E. Verhine and Peter S. White

Thomas J. La Belle

Dedicated to my teachers Sally Newman, Christina Paulston, Rolland Paulston, and John Singleton

Christopher R. Ward

Contents

Introduction

In this era of increasing diversity on college and university campuses, faculty, staff, and administrators are having to continually assess what they are doing to prepare students to know, appreciate, and interact in a world of ethnic and racial complexity. It is a world where individual and group identity and the relations among cultural groups and social classes are assuming unprecedented importance in setting the course of nations and their citizens. Educators are asking themselves whether students are graduating with the linguistic, interpersonal, and intellectual expertise which will enable them to feel comfortable and productive in a global society. Even more, perhaps, is the desire that graduates be proactive in establishing the kinds of interdependent and mutually supportive relations that the world seeks as it enters the twenty-first century.

Because higher education is inextricably linked to the larger society which surrounds and permeates it, colleges and universities mirror the issues and concerns that are part of daily living. Thus, when the larger society is showing signs of strain along racial, ethnic, gender, and, among others, social class lines, those same strains appear inside libraries and classrooms. In many respects, the pursuit of educational change inside institutions does not and cannot proceed without attention to the controversies and conflicts which characterize what is going on outside. Thus, as people line up on issues like affirmative action, the rights of gays and lesbians, abortion, religion in schools, and sexual harassment, they inevitably permeate the thin veneer which administratively separates schooling from the rest of society.

Diversity in the United States has been and will remain a major issue affecting identity, behavior, and public policy. In that regard, this book addresses one of the major questions of the 1990s and beyond, namely, "How do colleges and universities best prepare students for common citizenship in a diverse, democratic state while also nurturing their groups' cultures, values, and institutional participation?" In dealing with this question, we attempt to step back from the issues to provide a historical and conceptual introduction to ethnicity, to multiculturalism, and to ethnic studies within the social and political constraints of the United States in the mid-nineties. Because that history and

1

framework often goes beyond higher education and builds on, or responds to, elementary and secondary education, we draw from relevant experiences and issues at those levels as well (see, for example, LaBelle and Ward, 1994). We also attempt to provide a framework for assessing alternative paths for changing higher education institutions to achieve diversity goals.

Our focus is on ethnic studies and multiculturalism, concepts and initiatives which in some instances are competing for attention in higher education institutions and in others are seen as complementary and mutually supportive. With ethnic studies, for example, there is attention given to a single ethnic group, typically because of local or regional population size or because of the existence of a critical interest in that group among faculty and students on a campus. The pursuit of the ethnic studies approach sets the precedent on a campus for other specific ethnic group study to follow, such that as demand grows from students, faculty, and community members new ethnic studies programs can be anticipated. With multicultural studies, the strategy is different. Here, the effort is typically more thematic and comparative rather than ethnic specific. In multicultural studies the goal is typically to infuse the curriculum within several departments and colleges with a variety of themes and issues drawn from across ethnic and racial groups. The extent to which such infusion is planned in a coherent and systematic way as opposed to a grab bag of courses chosen from a list volunteered by faculty varies across campuses.

The results of these two strategies are also different. Once established, for example, an ethnic studies program typically has department status, with a minimum core of faculty and a group of student majors and minors pursuing the field as in any other discipline or profession. Beyond the major and minor, the role played by ethnic studies in the provision of general education courses varies in accord with its desire to reach out to other students, along with the acceptability of its courses to faculty colleagues. In some instances an ethnic studies program is by choice isolated and in others it leads the campus in diversity programs. In the case of multicultural studies, the organizational framework is most likely interdisciplinary, with a scattering of conceptually focused or disparate courses and faculty placed across the campus. It is not likely that there are many institutions where students are majoring in multiculturalism. Instead, there are many where there is a basic commitment to providing coursework which contributes to the liberal education of undergraduates, and in some instances, to those entering the professions.

In many respects, these two strategies, as outlined above, are not competitive when it comes to goals and populations served. Thus, to us, ethnic studies and multiculturalism often make natural partners in efforts to increase attention to diversity issues. They are sometimes competitive, however, such as in a climate of tight budget conditions where institutions are pressed to choose which effort deserves to retain or secure additional resources. Further, as we will argue, they are often competitive substantively and philosophically. Fiscally, administrators must determine the long-range implications of building a core faculty to serve a relatively limited number of majors and minors in an ethnic studies program. Benefits increase if an ethnic studies program also offers service courses to a general education undergraduate population. An investment in multicultural education, however, while it may serve a wider general studies population and be more effective at infusing cross-cultural issues into the curriculum across a campus, may not result in any focused or in-depth capabilities for students or faculty at an institution. Furthermore, multicultural studies does not respond to the political and social pressure to make relevant an institution's curriculum to the presence of a critical mass of students from one or more ethnic groups.

Substantively, ethnic studies and multicultural studies are also different and both have their supporters and detractors. In addition to the depth-versus-breadth arguments supporting the former and latter respectively, there are other issues which are implicit in the approaches. Perhaps the major one revolves around the extent to which ethnic studies and multicultural studies are used to support separatism and independence among and between groups as opposed to inclusion and interdependence. Another way of thinking about the issue is the extent to which such programs bring people together for nationalism and unity as opposed to reinforcing group identity and some degree of isolation by building on linguistic, cultural, or other ties. As we will suggest, we believe that there exists substantial social space in most societies for group identity to be built and furthered without endangering the nation state or national traditions.

Because of the importance of these issues for aspiring and practicing educators, we have written this text with them in mind. Thus, this book is intended to serve two principal audiences, students and professionals on the job, whose major concern is higher education, educational administration, foundations of education, ethnic studies, and multicultural education. As a supplementary text, it will also be helpful to those teaching courses on ethnicity, ethnic studies or policies, and intergroup relations. For students, we hope to have provided an introduction to, and background for, the issues surrounding diversity in both society and educational institutions. For practicing professionals, we believe that the book will appeal to administrators, faculty, and student-service personnel who seek a relatively comprehensive and conceptually based (rather than a polemic or a "how to" manual) overview of how ethnic studies and multiculturalism fit into the current diversity debates in higher education. For them, the book will provide a perspective on the constraints on various approaches to ethnicity and diversity, and facilitate their being able to pursue alternative means for achieving institutional change.

The book is organized into three parts, each of which contains two chapters. In the first part, we introduce multiculturalism and education by initially laying out the historical developments prior to 1960 and then by introducing the concepts which we will use to guide our discussion in later chapters. In chapter 1, we focus on the antecedents of multiculturalism, beginning with access to higher education in the nineteenth century and by highlighting the ways in which formal education, especially primary and secondary schools, have interacted with differing ethnic and racial groups. Whether interacting with forced or voluntary immigrants, educators at all levels of schooling in the United States early on made efforts to forge a national identity. Sometimes this process went forth with programs to assimilate, typically under the direction of whites and in segregated institutions. In others, such assimilation was not pursued because it was deemed impossible or undesirable, or because efforts were made to build on rather than change cultural traditions and practices of learners. The first chapter documents how the early efforts at group studies and bilingual education were carried out and how several ethnic and racial groups struggled to gain access and find relevant their educational experiences.

In chapter 2, we introduce the terms *ethnicity*, *race*, and *social class* as social science concepts and labels and highlight the ways in which they are used as heuristic devices to guide the discussion of diversity. Attention is drawn to acculturation and assimilation as well as to how groups come together in society and work out both conflictual and harmonious relationships. We look at how educational institutions at all levels act as arenas within which these relations are typically tested and developed. Schooling is characterized as an institution that has assisted certain groups to gain access or maintain their status and identity while simultaneously serving as a vehicle for socializing others to accept a status and function determined for them.

The second section of the book brings contemporary multiculturalism and ethnic studies in higher education to the forefront by highlighting the first in chapter 3 and the second in chapter 4. Our treatment of multiculturalism in chapter 3 involves a broad-based review of the ways in which the term has been used since 1960, with special emphasis on usage in the 1980s. Our assessment indicates that the term itself is characterized by differing meanings, from preparing students for a diverse society to a mechanism for achieving societal change. We draw on case studies of institutions to demonstrate some of this variability, including attention to the issues which affect the implementation of programs and their interaction with ethnic studies. Our assessment uncovers the rather obvious lack of interaction between multiculturalism and international area studies, which we believe must be included if multiculturalism is to do justice to the reality of immigrant groups and their home connections.

Ethnic studies, the multicultural studies counterpart, is the subject of chapter 4. We trace the history of these programs from the 1960s to the 1990s by first pointing to some of the reasons for their emergence. Foremost among them is the demographic diversification of students in higher education. It was the access provided to a much more diverse student body which ultimately led to individual ethnic groups seeking representation of their cultural backgrounds in higher education curricula, administration, and faculty. The development of ethnic studies paralleled and interacted with the social issues of the day. Specifically, such programs were fueled by political protests at the time of the Civil Rights movement and the war in Vietnam. Ethnic studies programs are characterized as having had a bumpy and difficult history. Their efforts to secure greater academic legitimacy while maintaining the social and political activism which accounted for their origins have often been frustrated. Further, each of the ethnic group programs discussed, including African American, Chicano, American Indian and Asian American, remain challenged, one or more by internal theoretical and knowledge-base divisions, by increased heterogeneity in their constituencies, by the need to maintain a critical mass of students and faculty on campuses, and all by struggles to secure the resources to maintain viability.

Our last two chapters in the third part of the book raise both the constraints and the potential strategies for furthering ethnic and multicultural studies. In chapter 5 we argue that it is difficult for higher education to be independent from the corresponding social and political pressures and constraints of the day. And in the mid-1990s, as we see them, the context is not favorable for furthering such efforts. Our assessment finds that the social and political landscape is filled with increased intergroup competition and conflict, to some extent over whose history and whose identity will be represented in higher education, and to some extent over issues like affirmative action and political correctness, which tend to cast a conservative pall over institutional initiatives. The challenges are many, emanating from demographic change, struggles over control of curricula, the political climate, the courts, religious groups, and so on, all of which tend to test the mettle of academic administrators as they make difficult investment and policy choices. This chapter sets the stage for the final chapter of the book by establishing the backdrop for a discussion of change strategies.

In chapter 6, we turn to the question of how to develop strategies to implement programs to prepare students for a diverse society. We argue that it is appropriate to explore the melding of ethnic and multicultural studies even though at some institutions the relationships are contentious. Our assessment suggests that while there are many obstacles to furthering studies which provide students with the skills and knowledge needed to participate in a diverse society, there are ways to address them. The question is how to turn the obstacles into catalysts for change, and we find that there is some momentum, despite the constraints, which offer promise. Among them is focusing resources on common conceptual frameworks for courses included in a multicultural initiative, highlighting the conflicts which surround multicultural issues, concentrating on selected themes which cut across groups, and taking a holistic approach to ethnic studies in addition to or rather than concentrating on a single group. Following a discussion of pedagogy we turn to the extracurricular area of higher education to explore the potential of complementing and supplementing the formal curriculum through activities which reside in student organizations, developmental education programs, resident halls, and the day-to-day social climate of a campus.

Part 1

Historical and Conceptual Backdrop

Ethnicity, Multiculturalism, and Higher Education in the United States Prior to 1960

The development of ethnic studies and multiculturalism and their relationship within various levels of formal education in the United States have been the subject of much discussion and debate in recent years. However, little attention has been paid to historical developments that shaped these movements prior to 1960.

Subordinate racial and ethnic groups had to contend with grossly unequal access to education and a lack of control over the educational institutions in which they participated. Well into the twentieth century, group-specific educational efforts such as the historically Black colleges faced issues that were to reemerge as ethnic studies developed in the 1960s. One such issue was whether ethnic groups should focus primarily on developing group-centered education or pursue access to white-dominated higher education. A second issue related to whether the curricula should emphasize preparing students for success in a white-dominated society and economy or inculcate them in group history and traditions, while preparing them for careers that served group needs.

During the same era, the roots of the current emphasis on multiculturalism developed in efforts such as bilingual schools and denominational colleges that used education to preserve subordinate-group culture and language. Many of these early efforts developed among groups of white European origin that had some degree of power and status.

In many early group-specific educational efforts, religion and religious organizations were important components. In some cases, such as Roman Catholic universities, religion served to differentiate between groups. In other cases, religious organizations played a supportive role. Protestant contributions to the development of historically Black colleges are an example of such support. Finally, religion and religious organizations sometimes played a negative role, with Christianity serving as the rationale for attacks on group culture and missionary organizations providing government-financed educational services.

Building on these earlier roots, post–World War II social, political, and demographic changes propelled a dramatic transformation of higher education from the late 1950s through the 1960s. These changes still shape the development and relationship of ethnic studies and multiculturalism in the nation's colleges and universities.

Unequal Access to Higher Education

Through most of the history of the United States, access to higher education has not been equally available to all groups. At one extreme, access was legally denied to African Americans solely on the basis of race. From 1896, when the Supreme Court ruled in favor of the "separate but equal" doctrine, to the mid-1930s, African Americans were excluded by law from all white colleges in the South. They continued to be denied admission to public universities in some states until well into the 1960s. Other groups faced similar legal barriers. Chinese Americans, for example, fought for integrated elementary and secondary public education in San Francisco and other parts of California in the late nineteenth and early twentieth centuries (Low, 1982).

Even when clear legal admission restrictions did not exist, African American access was limited by other means, including school policies and cultures that made it clear that African Americans were not welcome. For example, in the 1920s Harvard still did not allow African American students to live in dormitories with white students (Kennedy, 1993). The limitations on access were effective. From 1865 to 1895 only 194 Blacks graduated from Northern colleges and 75 of these were from Oberlin (Bowles and De Costa, 1971).

For some groups, such as Jews, access was limited more sporadically. Able to enter urban public universities such as City College of New York, Jews were often denied access to elite private institutions such as Princeton and other Ivy League schools. Unable to deny entry on the basis of scholarship, these establishment colleges and universities instituted character tests and psychological exams as part of their admissions requirements. Quotas were also used to limit Jewish admissions. After an unspoken quota took effect at Columbia University in the 1920s, Jewish enrollment dropped from 40 to 22 percent in two years. During the same period Harvard was still publicly discussing limiting Jewish enrollment (Steinberg, 1974).

Native Americans, Hispanics, women, and other groups, as well as those lacking financial resources or acceptable formal secondary education, have also had limited access to higher education in the United States. In some cases, group values have served to limit access when subordinate groups felt that public education was not suitable for their children. Steinberg (1974) argues that such was the case with nineteenth-century American Roman Catholics, who developed a comprehensive educational system of their own. In other cases, groups have found that once achieved, access to higher education is not continually assured. For example, the internment of American citizens of Japanese descent during World War II disrupted higher education for their children, who prior to the war had reached levels of formal educational achievement equal to or exceeding those of the general population (Daniels, 1988).

Group-Specific Education

As one response to limited access to education in the nineteenth century, some white religious and ethnic groups in the United States established separate institutions and systems of higher education. In addition to providing higher education when none could be had elsewhere, these colleges and universities served to preserve group languages, cultures, and traditions. Moreover, in contrast to African Americans and Native Americans, the white ethnic groups controlled, for the most part, their institutions and their administration and curriculum. Among these institutions were the colleges and universities run by the Roman Catholic Church and the Protestant liberal arts colleges begun by various immigrant groups, such as the Scandinavians in the upper Midwest.

Few in number until the Irish immigration of the mid–nineteenth century, Roman Catholics had been secure in areas of French and Spanish colonization. In fact, the first schools in what are now the United States were Catholic schools in Florida, New Mexico, and California. However, when English power prevailed in colonial America, Protestantism, not Catholicism, benefitted, establishing a pattern of Protestant domination in education.

Until the first Catholic college (Georgetown) was founded in 1789, English colonial colleges from Harvard to the University of Charleston were uncompromisingly Protestant. Anti-Catholic sentiments remained until the twentieth century, with some colonies (Maryland, for example) passing eighteenth-century laws against Catholics running schools (Power, 1972). Of the 182 colleges established before the Civil War, 175 were subject to denominational control. Of these, 28 were Catholic. These early Catholic colleges were established to prepare priests and to ensure the moral formation of Catholic youth (Power, 1972). By the twentieth century, Catholic higher education grew into a nationwide system, and Catholics entered public higher education in large numbers, eventually reaching attendance rates equal to those for the general population. However, the inequality of access remained much greater for African Americans, Native Americans, and Chicanos.

For African Americans, separate institutions provided access to higher education when dominant white institutions were closed to them. However, unlike Catholic and Protestant immigrants from Europe, African Americans did not control the system of colleges and universities that enrolled them and that came to be known as historically Black institutions. In reality, most of these institutions' faculty, administration, and boards were controlled or heavily influenced by whites, reflecting a situation in nineteenth-century education where European immigrants, lower-class whites, and Blacks fought for intellectual, social, economic, and political advancement, but where Blacks remained in the most subordinate position (Berry and Blassingame, 1982).

As we prepare to consider ethnic studies programs and their emergence in the 1960s, it is instructive to consider the development and changes in the system of African American higher education from before the Civil War through the middle of the twentieth century. First, however, it should be noted that during the same period no similar system of higher education developed for other groups, specifically Native Americans (Brubacher and Rudy, 1976), whose relation to higher education we shall trace later in the chapter. Likewise, no separate higher education system developed for Asian Americans. Many of the first Asian immigrants were Chinese males, and as other groups (Japanese, Koreans, and Filipinos) followed the Chinese, their struggles were first with equal access to elementary and secondary education and later with the right to maintain their own language schools (Daniels, 1988).

The system of African American higher education that emerged in the mid–nineteenth century was characterized by

- largely private institutions until well into the twentieth century
- white dominance in faculty, administration, and boards
- declining northern liberal support and growing influence from industrial philanthropists
- splits over approaches to the curriculum linked to sources of funding and to visions of African Americans' role in society.

Throughout the development of the system, some African Americans entered white-dominated institutions. Their numbers remained small until the 1930s, when the major thrust for change turned from reliance on institutional improvement, accreditation, and growing student enrollment to legal battles for increased access to all institutions, particularly to state-funded professional and graduate schools.

Institutions of higher education for African Americans emerged in a few scattered locations before the Civil War. Although the system of higher education for African Americans was almost exclusively a southern phenomenon, with 90 percent of American Blacks residing in the South in 1900, some of the first individual institutions were in the North. Lincoln University in Pennsylvania, founded in 1854, and Wilberforce University in Ohio, founded in 1856, were the first colleges established for blacks.

Other higher education efforts trained African Americans as teachers and ministers prior to 1854. For example, as early as 1831, abolitionists and members of the Convention of the Free People of Color attempted to establish a college in New Haven. Opposed by the city's citizens, the Convention selected another site in New Hampshire, where the town quickly removed the academy. Finally, in 1842 the Institute for Colored Youth was established in Philadelphia; this eventually became Cheyney State University (Bowles and De Costa, 1971).

At the end of the Civil War, 4.5 million African Americans were freed from slavery. With the passage of the fourteenth and fifteenth amendments, they received citizenship and the right to vote. This freedom released a pent-up demand for basic education and an accompanying need for trained teachers for elementary and secondary schools. This demand for teachers, in turn, created the need for higher education institutions to train them.

During the three decades following the Civil War the development and growth of the system of historically Black colleges and universities was generally funded by private monies and supported by private interests, especially Protestant churches. Missionary organizations, both those supported by African Americans and those supported by northern whites, founded many of the historically Black colleges between 1865 and 1890 (Bowles and De Costa, 1971).

Initially, some public support for African American higher education came from the federal government's Freedman's Bureau. The Bureau often worked with churches and did so to help found Howard University. However, as northern interest in the education of freed slaves waned, the Bureau ended its involvement with higher education in 1872 (Brubacher and Rudy, 1976). At the same time, southern legislatures, with the backing of industrialists eager for workers, appropriated money for vocational institutes for Blacks, but not for liberal arts institutions.

Public financial support for African American higher education during this period was meager; when financing did come it was in the form of the Second Morrill (land grant) Act. After Congress passed the original Morrill Act in 1862, states established land-grant colleges, but these were nearly all institutions from which Blacks were excluded. Before 1890, only Alcorn State in Mississippi, Hampton University, and Claflin University in South Carolina received 1862 land-grant funds (Humphries, 1992).

The 1890 Second Morrill Act confirmed the "separate but equal" philosophy that the Supreme Court would rule in *Plessy v. Ferguson* in 1896. By

1897, sixteen of the seventeen states that maintained separate systems of education had established a state-supported land-grant college for blacks. During their first few decades these institutions enrolled large numbers of secondary students and the institutions struggled to establish bachelor degree programs. By the 1950s, the colleges were still emphasizing teacher training and lacked resources to train students as researchers, engineers, and other professionals (Humphries, 1992).

Throughout the latter part of the nineteenth century and into the twentieth, whites dominated Black college administrations, faculties, and boards. Many whites, having lost the zeal of Reconstruction, were domineering and paternalistic. Whites withheld or granted financial support as a means of institutional control (Berry and Blassingame, 1982).

Intensifying the impact of this control was a decrease in funding from the liberal northern churches which had founded and initially funded many of the colleges. During the latter part of the nineteenth century, the South's primary economic interest for cheap, docile labor merged with that of northern industrial philanthropists who were becoming increasingly important as funders of African American higher education. Like many persons in the South, the northern industrialists favored education that prepared African Americans for manual labor and undergirded the economy.

By the early twentieth century, African Americans began calling for control of Black higher education. These calls peaked in the 1920s with student demonstrations and strikes at Hampton Institute, Howard University, and Fisk. Only in 1925 did Mordecai Johnson became the first Black president of Howard (Berry and Blassingame, 1982).

Even as African Americans fought for control of the institutions where they were enrolled, they also sought access to all institutions of higher education. In the 1930s, the NAACP led the assault on segregated white universities, first targeting graduate and professional schools. In southern states that did not provide graduate and professional training for African Americans, the NAACP argued this lack of training was prima facie evidence that facilities provided by the states to whites and Blacks were not equal and therefore unconstitutional. In 1938, the Supreme Court ruled that the state of Missouri was denying equal educational opportunity by giving a Black person a scholarship to attend a law school in another state. In response, southern states began building graduate facilities for Blacks. However, in 1950 the Court held that a separate law school for Blacks in Texas was not equal. Although the University of Maryland Law School was desegregated in 1935 and West Virginia University admitted a Black graduate student without compulsion in 1940, in 1952 five states still barred Black students from their publicly supported universities (Berry and Blassingame, 1982; Brubacher and Rudy, 1976).

During the latter part of the nineteenth century and into the twentieth, a debate raged within the African American community about the purpose of higher education. At issue was the thrust of the curriculum of the African American colleges. The two major figures in the debate were Booker T. Washington, who promoted an ideal of industrial education based on manual labor and self-help, and W. E. B. DuBois, who supported a liberal arts education.

Washington was identified first with Hampton Institute, from which he graduated, and then with Tuskegee Institute, which he built up. His primary goal was to teach people how to make a living, and the Hampton-Tuskegee industrial-education program favored practical skills like masonry with lesser emphasis on basic academic skills.

Though popular with some, Washington's industrial-education approach was rejected by much of the African American leadership. From the 1870s through the 1920s many African American newspapers, conventions, and writers fought against it. These groups felt African Americans needed to know more about themselves and acquaint whites with African American achievement. Thus, liberal arts colleges continued to dominate the education of African Americans, and colleges such as Fisk and Howard were viewed as institutions to impart the elite northern Protestant culture to African American youth. However, African Americans began to modify this philosophy to include the scientific study of Black life and culture, as DuBois had successfully inaugurated at Atlanta University in 1900 and as Carter G. Woodson initiated with the founding of the *Journal of Negro History* in 1916 (Anderson, 1988).

These diverse views of higher education held by Washington, DuBois, and their supporters were not simple differences in opinion. The educational approaches were tied to differing visions of the role that African Americans should play in American society. One vision emphasized the necessity for all African Americans to learn basic industrial or vocational skills. The other saw this vocational emphasis as too limited and maintained that education should develop the group's leadership. Furthermore, each vision was linked to specific sources of financial support in an era when northern philanthropists' funding of African American higher education increased while funding from the liberal missionary and Black church organizations decreased.

The northern philanthropists saw higher education as most appropriately an industrial education, exemplified by the Hampton-Tuskegee idea. They further saw it as an ideological force that would prepare teachers to help African Americans adjust to a subordinate social role in the South, a role favorable to their own economic interests. Beginning in the 1880s, northern philanthropy placed almost total emphasis on industrial training. In support of this thrust, the various foundation funds (General Education Board, Phelps-Stokes Fund, Carnegie Foundation, Laura Spelman Rockefeller Memorial Fund) cooperated on behalf of the Hampton-Tuskegee program.

In contrast, missionary leadership objected to the Hampton-Tuskegee model, which they viewed as undermining the democratic rights of African Americans. On this issue, the African American leadership and that of the religious organizations agreed: "Despite sharp tension between missionaries and black leaders over questions of Black participation in the administration and faculty of missionary colleges, the two groups shared a common conception of the appropriate training of Black leaders" (Anderson, 1988, p. 244). They both saw future leadership for the African American community being trained in a classical curriculum.

Throughout the development of the African American system of higher education, academic quality was a major issue. Many of the colleges evolved as institutions of higher education after decades as primary and secondary institutions. The separate system of public education for Blacks created a great demand for trained teachers, although not necessarily teachers with four-year college degrees. This demand for teachers—however badly they were treated and paid—drew students into the Black colleges. Thus, the colleges were at once part of the system of black education and also shapers of it (Bowles and De Costa, 1971).

The institutions faced significant structural problems when large numbers of students arrived lacking sufficient academic preparation for college-level work. The emphasis on production of teachers and other basic professionals needed by the African American community, rather than on the training of engineers, researchers, and other professionals, influenced the colleges well into the middle of the twentieth century. Moreover, the Black system was, on one hand, completely dependent on the white system for support—a system that blatantly discriminated against it; on the other hand, the Black system was completely separate, with standards determined internally and each system training its own teachers.

In the 1920s the first accreditation was made of Black colleges by the Southern Association of Colleges and Secondary Schools. This began the removal of one barrier to graduates of Black colleges. But others remained, including the severe limits on the professions Black college graduates could enter. For example, into the 1950s the United States Post Office remained the largest employer of educated African Americans, reflecting the barriers in the nongovernment labor market faced by those who managed to attain a college degree in the 1920s, 1930s, and 1940s.

Bowles and De Costa (1971) see significant improvements in the colleges from the early 1930s through 1953 in large part because of the regional accrediting agencies. Moreover, the accreditation process forced southern politicians to comply with court decisions. Legislatures realized that accredited white colleges and nonaccredited Black colleges would be judged as evidence of noncompliance with the separate-but-equal ruling.

Further improvements in the system came as a result of World War I, better economic fortunes in the South, and the growth of military bases in the South. From within the African American community came higher demand for education, calls for higher standards, demand for better-educated Black teachers, and the development of Black colleges. Also the children of persons who had migrated north became a source of students for the Black system as parents and children discovered the discrimination against them in the North and its institutions.

During the 1930s, the progress of African American higher education was mixed. Physical facilities improved but the dependence on northern philanthropy with its desire for conservative African American leadership continued. African American intellectuals in the 1930s began to talk about the miseducation of Black youth and the increasing distance between the educated Black youth and most Black Americans. The youth were seen as internalizing the social ideology of the industrial philanthropists. Black college administrators were caught in the middle, between the criticism leveled against them and the need for funding to survive (Anderson, 1988).

Throughout the second half of the nineteenth and the first half of the twentieth century, limited numbers of African American students attended white institutions. African Americans' acceptance by Oberlin, Berea, and other colleges was one of the first steps in ending the proscription against Blacks entering higher education. However, for the small number who did enter white-dominated institutions, life was not easy. Berry and Blassingame (1982) emphasize the tribulations Black students faced, including financial difficulties, but also cite the students' perseverance and emphasize how success was a consciousness-raising experience that shattered forever their acceptance of whites' characterization of blacks as inferior.

This growing realization that even as formal segregation ended in higher education there remained a great deal of racism and many obstacles for African Americans became one basis for the protests of the 1960s and the founding of ethnic studies programs. It merged with long-standing concerns about the relationship of various educational approaches to the needs of the community and with early efforts to develop the study of the African American experience to contribute to the development of African American studies.

Native American Education

The preceding section showed the development of a separate system of higher education enrolling African Americans and the parallel struggle of African Americans for greater access to dominant-group colleges and universities, and linked this development to the emergence of ethnic studies. We turn now to another example of group-specific education, that of Native Americans. Their experience demonstrates how education has been used by dominant groups in the United States to devalue subordinate groups' cultures and then to reshape those groups' cultures, religious commitment, and national identification. On another level, the history of Native American education shows the almost complete lack of access Native Americans had to higher education—particularly to education they controlled—through the middle of the twentieth century. The response after 1960 has been both the growth of Native American studies and the establishment of tribally controlled community colleges.

Educational historian Joel Spring (1994) describes American government policies toward conquered peoples, including those toward Native Americans and Puerto Ricans, as ones of deculturalization and Americanization. Propelling these various policies, particularly in the nineteenth century, has been the superiority white European Americans felt about their country, its place in the world, and its future—its "manifest destiny."

Spring sees these policies demonstrated in two massive education campaigns to replace Native American languages and cultures with English and European culture. One campaign was associated with the forced removal in the 1830s of Native Americans from the southeastern United States to west of the Mississippi; the second was the late-nineteenth-century removal of individual Native American children from their families to send them off to white-run boarding schools.

These campaigns were followed by a brief period in the 1920s and 1930s when the government supported restoration of native cultures; later, the policy turned to tribal termination and assimilation into dominant culture in the 1940s and 1950s. The demands of the 1960s and 1970s for Native American control of their own educational institutions grew from this history (Spring, 1994).

From the arrival of the first colonists in New England in the early seventeenth century, Native Americans were the focus of dominant-group pressures for cultural and religious change. The Protestant English immigrants sought to use schooling to Christianize and "civilize" Native Americans, as well as to pacify them. Included in these activities was the inculcation of English culture, with demands that Native American children adhere to many details of its standards of appearance and rituals of daily behavior. It was an approach that was based more on the colonists' sense of cultural superiority than on a belief in racial superiority.

This early approach of the New England Protestants established the patterns often repeated later in white-controlled Native American education: culturally intolerant goals which focused on a fusion of Christianity and Western secular values; a belief in the potential of Native Americans for "uplift"; a faith in the schools as a means to carry out this process; an educational approach that combined physical labor, secular instruction, and religious instruction; and the separation of Native American children from relatives and culture (Coleman, 1993).

The colonists', and later the United States government's approach to Native Americans was based on a variety of motives. Some whites seemed genuinely concerned about the disappearance of Native Americans, particularly in the face of growing colonial expansion. By the late eighteenth and early nineteenth centuries, officials in the new United States government who held this view worked to protect Native Americans from the worst of what they saw as the inevitable onslaught of European civilization. Reflecting concern for a civilizing mission over a strictly pacifying mission was the transfer of Native American affairs from the War Department to a unit of that department, the Bureau of Indian Affairs (BIA), in 1824, and the BIA's transfer to the Interior Department in 1849.

Those who sought to keep Native American tribes from disappearing, while at the same time not challenging white expansion onto Native American lands, proposed to make Native Americans Christians and farmers through support for missionary schools. The result was an unusual alliance between church and state that continued throughout much of the nineteenth century. Even after the Civil War, the government continued to turn responsibility for Native American education over to churches until 1876, when government schools began to expand. The American Board of Commissioners for Foreign Missionaries (ABCFM—founded in 1810 by Presbyterians and Congregationalists) provided teachers and the Civilization Fund Act (1819) and Indian treaty monies provided the financial support. The practical effect was that the government hired Protestant—and later Roman Catholic—churches to carry out the education of Native Americans.

However, despite apparent concern for tribal survival, the goal of the ABCFM schools was to rid Native American children of their traditions and to transform them into cultural copies of white children. The ABCFM schools' curricula totally excluded Native American culture and the ABCFM, like earlier colonists, viewed the situation as one of Native Americans either civilizing or perishing.

Prior to the educational efforts that emerged out of concern that Native Americans might be wiped out, some whites saw them as the subjects of dominant-group education, including the earliest higher education efforts in the colonies. A limited number of Native Americans attended colleges, including Harvard, Princeton, Dartmouth, and the College of William and Mary, from the seventeenth century. Some colleges were established with specific policies of admitting Native Americans.

These efforts were, for the most part, failures. For example, schooling of Native Americans was one of the first objectives of Harvard University according to its charter of 1650; the second building built on the campus was known as Indian College. However, only a few Native Americans lived in the hall and only one Native American graduated from Harvard in the seventeenth century (Oppelt, 1990; Stein, 1992).

Some support for Native American education came from abroad. Monies in the estate of Englishman Robert Boyle (founder of modern chemistry) were designated for the education of Native Americans, including funds to the College of William and Mary. By 1712, twenty Indian students were enrolled at the college. The Revolutionary War led to a cutoff of funds for these efforts (Oppelt, 1990).

Dartmouth was the first college founded for the education of Native Americans. Despite the statement in its charter that it was for the "education and instruction of youth of the Indian tribes," it never enrolled many Native Americans. In fact, prior to 1793, fewer than one hundred Native Americans attended Dartmouth, and only eight graduated in the nineteenth century. In the century from 1865 to 1965, twenty-eight Native Americans enrolled at Dartmouth and nine graduated (Oppelt, 1990).

At another level, academies—a new form of school to prepare men for medicine, politics, and teaching—appeared in the latter part of the eighteenth century. Academies demonstrated the same pattern followed by the colleges, including openness to Native Americans followed by almost exclusive enrollment of whites. Several academies were founded for Native Americans. One of these academies, Oneida, initially enrolled Native Americans, but soon became Hamilton College, for whites.

The forced removal of Native Americans from the Southeast involved the tribes who eventually came to assume the most control over their own educational institutions. The Choctaw and Cherokee were forcefully moved from the southeastern United States to what was later to be the state of Oklahoma. Before and after the move, the Choctaw and Cherokee had high levels of tribal-run education, including schools and bilingual education efforts. However, illustrating the dilemma facing subordinate groups in an economy dominated by the values and technologies of others, their schools taught agricultural and domestic tasks needed to change to a white-style economy (Oppelt, 1990).

The Choctaws felt that education was vital to their survival; they also supported the idea of developing a written language. Choctaws established an educational system in collaboration with missionaries, in which the best graduates were sent on to college. For example, the Choctaw Academy in Kentucky was established using money from treaty funds. It was the most advanced formal schooling available to Native Americans in this period and enrolled over 150 at its high point. For twenty years the Academy was the most significant Indian educational institution in the United States. The Academy had both church and government support and significant Choctaw leadership (Oppelt, 1990).

In Oklahoma, Cherokees used bilingual teachers and Cherokee texts to produce a literacy rate of nearly 100 percent. Western Oklahoma Cherokees had a higher literacy level in English than did the white population of Texas or Arkansas. However, in 1899 the government began taking over the tribal educational system and did so by 1901, turning its nearly two hundred schools into vocational training schools. Within twenty years of the takeover of their schools, the Cherokee literacy rate dropped to 40 percent (DeJong, 1993).

The Cherokees supported higher education. For example, the Cherokee National Council opened national male and female seminaries in 1851. These opened and closed periodically in the nineteenth century, graduating 382 men and 252 women from 1855 to 1909. These tribal institutions were eventually purchased by the state of Oklahoma. One became Northeastern Oklahoma State University. Other schools, church-related, were established for Indian education but became white universities—the University of Tulsa is an example.

The off-reservation boarding schools—Carlisle in Pennsylvania was the first and most famous—became an important instrument for whites to replace native languages with English, to destroy Indian culture among children, and to teach allegiance to the U.S. government. The schools had an English-only policy and flew the American flag to develop patriotism.

In perhaps the best known of the boarding school pedagogical innovations, Native American students worked for whites a few months each year to earn money and to learn about white life. The goals of this work were to develop students' individualism and in other ways enculturate them with the dominant-group culture by getting them away from other Native Americans. The schools also used extracurricular activities to develop model American citizens from members of various tribes. Carlisle, for example, maintained an extensive athletic program, regularly competing against major colleges in football and producing several Olympic athletes (Coleman, 1993).

In 1887 there were eight boarding schools enrolling 2137 people. The schools remained preeminent in federal Indian education until 1930, and some continued to operate into the 1980s. Although their goals were assimilationist, the boarding schools did not succeed very well. Most graduates returned to tribes with skills they could not use and with cultural values that put them outside both the Native American and the white worlds. Academically, the boarding schools were, at best, on level with a good vocational high school. In some cases, however, such schools had serious problems and inspectors found poor food and paramilitary types of organization.

By the beginning of the twentieth century, the concern for the survival of Native American peoples that had guided white supporters of Native American education was replaced by a more racially motivated outlook. Whites increasingly saw Native Americans as unable to learn and the curriculum moved more toward vocationalism. Less emphasis was placed on complex vocational skills and on anything academic. Racism and a concept of Native American inferiority became more prevalent.

However, within several decades of these discouraging developments came another swing in the approach to Native American education. In 1928, a national government report (the Meriam Report) was highly critical of Indian education. The report noted that Native Americans needed to have their own tribal, social, and civic life to use as the basis for understanding their place in society. In response, the BIA first tried to build a flexible curriculum that put positive value on Indian lifestyles. Native Americans, however, still did not control their own institutions. Immediately after World War II, the efforts to design education based on Native American's own institutions and values declined as the government emphasized the termination of tribes.

There was a small amount of federal aid for Native American higher education in the 1930s. By 1933, 161 Native Americans had enrolled in college with the aid of federal and tribal funds, and a few institutions offered scholarships to individuals. In addition, a handful of Native American–controlled colleges, mostly church-run, survived. Among these was Bacone College, the oldest Native American college in the United States. Founded as the Baptist University of Indians in 1889 to train teachers and preachers for the Five Civilized Tribes, Bacone produced significant Native American leadership and until 1960s was the only predominantly Native American college in the United States. Efforts such as Bacone would continue in the 1980s and into the 1990s, with the opening of a series of Native American community colleges (Oppelt, 1990). Until the 1960s, Native American access to higher education remained pitifully small with the number of Native Americans graduating from four-year institutions rising from sixty-six in 1961 to almost triple that number in 1968 (Szasz, 1974).

The experience of many Native American men during World War II when they left their reservations to serve in the military and the opportunities afforded by the GI Bill had a major impact on their attitudes toward participation in and control of education. Beginning with the Navajo Community College in 1968, tribally controlled community colleges were established in a number of states. Federal recognition and support for these efforts came with the passage of the Tribally Controlled Community College Act in 1978 (Stein, 1992).

Group Preservation Efforts

Group-specific educational efforts have been common throughout the history of the United States. Among these efforts have been schools organized by immigrant groups and ethnic groups to preserve their languages and heritages, as well as efforts to assimilate groups into the dominant-group culture and economy. German bilingual education schools, private and public, were some of the most widespread and longest lasting of the institutions organized by immigrant groups to retain their culture while also fully participating in the wider American culture and economy. German bilingual education also illustrates how religion was associated with many groups' efforts to provide their own education, how most ethnic educational institutions declined as members assimilated, how the growth in the number of immigrant groups in the late nineteenth and early twentieth century increased demands for access to schools for language and other instruction, and how events beyond the United States—particularly the World Wars—affected American's attitudes about assimilation and, hence, school enrollment. Carolyn Toth (1990) describes the history of German bilingual education with particular emphasis on the public German bilingual schools in Cincinnati, Ohio. This large bilingual program operated successfully for more than seventy-five years until halted by World War I anti-German hysteria.

German immigrants established schools in the United States to teach English and German with the expectation that students would use both languages for the rest of their lives. In this respect they were different from contemporary transitional bilingual education programs which seek to move students from their mother tongue into English as quickly as possible. It is also important to note that as a group Germans could not be considered as having subordinate status and did not have to contend with the racially based exclusion and slavery that African Americans experienced or the cultural exclusion and status as a defeated indigenous people faced by Native Americans. Like many group-specific schools, and unlike current public bilingual efforts, the German bilingual schools were founded for religious purposes. German immigrants saw that, in America, speaking English was often an economic necessity, but that English was used for ordinary, daily activities. In contrast, they knew that German was the language of the scriptures and its maintenance a moral imperative. With education equated with religion, virtually all German sects established parochial schools.

In the colonial period, one sect, the Moravians, was the most active in setting up schools, in part because it received support from Europe and in part because it was involved in Native American education. In 1749, Moravians established prestigious bilingual boarding schools for boys in Nazareth and Bethlehem, Pennsylvania. Among other German groups, the German Reformed Church and the German Lutherans together founded hundreds of schools.

Throughout the nineteenth century, bilingual German-English schools spread among both Lutherans and Catholics. Lutheran parochial schools reached a peak of development in 1890 when they numbered almost two thousand, with the largest numbers in Wisconsin, Illinois, and Iowa. To provide teachers, the German Lutherans opened seminaries in Ohio, Iowa, Minnesota, and Illinois.

The German Catholics—who immigrated later, largely after 1870—were also active in bilingual education. The Roman Catholic Church initially lent support to retention of German. However, the Catholic hierarchy was Irish and less concerned about the language issue. This lack of emphasis was strengthened by a papal decree that children of immigrants could switch to English-speaking parishes when they became adults. Nevertheless, by 1886 there were 825 Catholic German schools enrolling 165,000 students in the United States. The Catholics also started German colleges and universities: St. Vincent College in Latrobe, Pennsylvania, opened in 1846, and St. John's University in Collegeville, Minnesota, in 1857.

The advent of public schools in the 1830s and 1840s altered, but did not stop, German bilingual education. In 1840 Germans in Cincinnati and other Ohio areas successfully pushed to get legal status for German in the state's public schools. As a result, in Cincinnati enrollment was widespread and the high numbers of students kept costs low, ensuring the program's survival. The number of German bilingual students in Cincinnati peaked at 18,000 in 1886, and in 1914 there were still 14,600.

Toth points out that many non-Germans received German instruction in the Cincinnati schools, including some African American students. To support the need for teachers, the German bilingual division of the Cincinnati Normal School was founded in 1871. At the outset, the Cincinnati program was truly bilingual, with a Anglo American teacher and a German American teacher splitting the instruction of each class. However, the amount of German language declined over time, and in the higher grades in 1870s only forty-five minutes a day was devoted to German.

Cincinnati was not the only city with German bilingual schools. In 1886, 150,000 students were enrolled in German bilingual schools in three hundred public school districts in twenty-five states. In Chicago, a majority of students in German bilingual schools were not German. By 1914, Germans were rapidly assimilating and the German language was being used less and less. Although six million Germans immigrated to the United States from 1820 to 1943, the largest number of any immigrant group, the number of arrivals dropped off after 1882.

The anti-German feelings that arose during World War I marked the end of the German bilingual education program in Cincinnati and had similar drastic effects on other bilingual and foreign language efforts. The Cincinnati program's enrollment plunged dramatically and the program closed in 1918 when Ohio banned the teaching of foreign languages in its elementary schools. Although the Supreme Court overturned this law in 1923, it was not until 1959 that foreign language instruction (mostly Spanish and French) started again in Cincinnati elementary schools. Ohio was not alone. In Minnesota, which at the outbreak of World War I had more than two hundred ethnic schools teaching German, Polish, French, Danish, Norwegian, and Dutch, foreign language teaching was banned in 1919.

Conclusion

With rising group expectations, an expanding and seemingly wealthier higher educational system, and more strident calls for racial justice, the stage was set by 1960 for increased attention to previously subordinated groups in U.S. higher education. As the number of African American, Hispanic, and other subordinate-group students grew on campuses, group interest turned from increasing access to increasing power within the universities. The issues of group control over institutions, programs, and curricula, prevalent since the nineteenth century, merged with newer calls for group studies programs and greater links between their communities and the colleges and universities. Later, in the 1980s and 1990s, other groups would advocate for multicultural education.

In this first chapter we have shown some of the historical events that shaped the rise and formation of the developments of the mid–twentieth century. For nearly a century prior to 1960, African Americans had struggled in a society where they were regularly and legally denied admission to many of the nation's colleges and universities. The system of Black colleges that arose to meet their needs was controlled by whites and experienced great curriculum debates linked to different visions of African Americans' role in society. These colleges also initiated efforts to study African American culture and history and convey it to the rest of the United States. Native Americans had even more limited access to higher education than did African Americans. The lack of Native American control over educational institutions contributed to education's use to remove Native American culture and to reshape youth in alien ways. In testimony to the importance of group control over education, tribes who shaped their own educational institutions, such as the Cherokee and the Choctaw, had greater success with formal education than those tribes which lacked control. Native American control in higher education was eventually established in Native American community colleges.

From the 1960s and into the 1990s other voices called for more diversity in higher education, honoring multiple voices and valuing participation by more groups. Here, the previous hundred years also showed examples of American educational diversity. Bilingual education, for example, thrived privately and publicly in major urban areas through the First World War. Catholics founded a large educational system that included colleges and universities throughout the United States. Asian Americans struggled both for the right of their children to attend integrated schools and for the right to maintain their own language schools. In chapter 3 we shall see how Intercultural Education sponsored programs and approaches in the 1940s and 1950s that valued diversity, and how they drew upon higher education for pedagogy, research, and theoretical underpinnings.

We turn now to some of these theoretical underpinnings, including the concepts of ethnicity, race, and social class.

CHAPTER 2

Segmentation and Intergroup Relations through Education

Both ethnic studies and multicultural education curricula are tied to concepts like ethnicity, race, and social class. Thus it is important that we devote attention to a general introduction to these terms and their use in providing a basis for the development of educational programs. In this chapter, we first discuss the use of ethnicity, race, and social class as labels and concepts to guide our later discussion of multicultural and ethnic studies. We then turn to how ethnic groups, racial groups, and social classes interact by looking at processes of acculturation and assimilation as well as the broader issue of intergroup relations and the economic, political, and social influences which shape them. Education, across all levels, is subsequently introduced as an important arena in which relations among groups are tested and shaped as each attempts to ensure that their particular values and interests are met. The chapter concludes with a discussion of how groups vie for control of the curricula as a way to influence the schooling process.

To begin, it is important to note that communication in the social sciences is facilitated by the use of concepts and terms which both label and explain human behavior. Terms like *social class*, *political*, and *psychological* are examples of labels which identify and provide guidance in explaining certain behavior. Others, like *ethnic* and *culture*, also serve to narrow the perceptual sphere by concentrating on a particular aspect of human behavior. In addition to labeling characteristics, social science terms are also used in an effort to explain behaviors. Thus, some behaviors may be linked causally to, among others, an individual's or group's position in the social structure, or on personality traits, political power, or occupational status.

As Thompson (1989) argues, this process of naming, labeling, and explaining behavior can be both difficult and somewhat arbitrary. He writes that labeling can be difficult because behaviors are complex and not likely to be easily classified, and because it is not always clear what can be associated with one particular social science label as opposed to another. Explanations may be even more problematic. Whether, for example, a behavior is primarily explained

27

through a social class or ethnic lens may be difficult to discern. Because of such issues, most would agree that a given behavior may be labeled and explained in several ways depending on its complexity and on the general context within which it is being manifested or observed. Another difficulty with using social science labels is that they can become stereotypes and self-fulfilling prophecies rather than simply a means for focusing attention. In such instances, members of an entire ethnic group may be stereotyped in negative ways. Individuals who can't find work, or who are on welfare, for example, might be stereotyped as lazy. This has happened with groups whose background is often characterized by poverty or high unemployment. The stereotype may persist even though the cause for unemployment may rest with the lack of jobs or with jobs which have little opportunity for advancement. Another example of stereotyping is labeling individuals who might adhere to certain religious beliefs as being fatalistic or unable to alter the course of their lives. Trying to overcome poverty or generations of oppression may provide more salient explanations for why a person believes he or she may not be able to shape the future.

Segmentation: Ethnicity, Race, and Social Class

While the negative implications of stereotyping following the labeling of behavior are significant, labeling nevertheless allows for organizing information and has the potential for increasing understanding of behavior. *Culture* has become such a label. It has evolved from its use in anthropology as a way to characterize the lifeways of a racial and ethnic population whose existence could be carved off and made independent from other groups, to a more general term implying some sharing of identity, goals, and status. In the traditional conceptions of culture, there may be attention to beliefs, technology, and social organization which together would make up the lifeways of that particular group. In more contemporary views of culture, almost any group of people who come together to fulfill any purpose can be said to have the potential of developing a culture. In this later case, *culture* means a group of people possessing some common understandings and characteristics—from membership criteria to the rules by which the group operates—to how the actual system which ties the individuals together functions as the group pursues its goals. It is this more contemporary view of culture which gives rise to the term's use as a reference to many different groups, from those characterized by occupational pursuits to the disabled, gays, lesbians, women, students, and so on. Although our primary interest is with ethnic groups, as they constitute the central concept underlying ethnic studies, we will use *culture* to refer to the commonalties which some believe set one group of individuals off from another.

Ethnicity

When we use the term *ethnic*, we mean a group of people who are said to have a common ancestry, memories of a shared past, and certain cultural behaviors (e.g., kinship, religion, language) which may set the members off from others and provide for group identity (Schermerhorn, 1970). It is assumed that the behavior is learned through membership in the ethnic group rather than inherited. Such learning results from close affiliation with an identifiable group and is typically seen in the language spoken, the beliefs and values held or manifested, or the ways in which individuals think about or make cognitive sense of their reality. These characteristics result from individuals identifying with others and sharing some similar experience. Similarity in adapting to certain physical environments or finding ways within those settings to meet survival needs in defined, accepted, and patterned ways are among the common experiences that bind members of a group. Such patterns are often reflected in the foods eaten, the clothing worn, and the vocabulary used to define and describe what is important and common in the environment. Within these patterns there is also variation. Thus, some behaviors, values, and beliefs may be central or common to most members of the community, while others may be found among smaller population segments. These differences among subgroups may be due to occupational pursuits, geographical location, political and religious affiliations, and so on.

Knowing an ethnic group is like having a road map as an abstract representation of a city or state. Thus, in one sense culture is an abstraction from reality. Cultural knowledge can also refer to actual behavior, however, and thus can serve as a guide to the ways in which life is conducted among a certain group—how people are born, are named, are carried, are taught to walk and talk, make the transition to adulthood, marry, and die and are buried. The cultural patterns underlying these behaviors are based on common understandings, on an organized way of thinking and acting, and on typical ways of relating to physical and material objects. Having the knowledge of a culture helps explain some, but certainly not all, of the behavior of the members of that culture. That's because, as indicated above, adherence to the patterns of culture are variable and determined by members of the particular group.

Barth (1969) argues that while defining an ethnic group through shared behaviors and values may be important, the most significant determinant of ethnicity is the extent to which members identify themselves and wish others to identify them as members of a group. He refers to these two dimensions as self-ascription and ascription by others. He points to both overt signals or signs—like dress, language, type of house lived in, or general lifestyle—which people look for and exhibit to show identity, as well as basic value orientations, standards of morality, and excellence by which performance is judged. In effect, because belonging to an ethnic group carries with it certain behavioral expectations and identity, it also carries with it a claim to be judged and to judge oneself by the criteria appropriate to that identity. This does not mean that behaviors will necessarily be the same across a group, since ethnic membership may be as directly tied to what a person says about the way he or she wishes to be treated and to have his or her behavior interpreted as to the way he or she acts. Thus, the celebration of uniqueness may be as much through pride in origins as it is through the celebration of those origins.

Social scientists are also finding that ethnic identity is becoming both more complex and more temporal. The complexity is pointed out by Waters (1990), who notes that ethnic identity can be both symbolic or influential, such as when an individual desires to participate in certain celebrations (e.g., St. Patrick's Day), and actual or salient. Ethnicity is also temporal because it can come and go, depending on acquaintances and the specific conditions (e.g., holidays) under which it is celebrated. Cross-ethnic and cross-racial relationships (see, for example, Wheeler, 1994) also complicate issues of identity, as those who represent mixed backgrounds may constitute a separate ethnic and racial category.

Race

The term *race* refers to an illusive concept used to classify human beings on the basis of certain hereditary characteristics. Because human beings are able to exchange physical and genetic qualities, however, there is an infinite variety of outward characteristics which separate the peoples of the world by physical type. This unbounded variety of human beings has led to a lack of agreement among scientists as to what constitutes an acceptable categorization of races. Although differing physical characteristics among people obviously exist, they are best seen as an overlapping continuum rather than sharp lines of distinction. Thus, dividing the human population into three major racial groups—Caucasoid, Mongoloid, and Negroid—is both arbitrary and difficult to determine.

Given the imprecise nature of race as the basis for group categorization, it is no surprise that controversy surrounds its linkage to social and personality differences. This is especially apparent in arguments which pit hereditary versus environmental influences on human behavior. While no one denies that both such genetic and social influences are interrelated in shaping individual behavior, some societies seem more concerned than others in demonstrating that one or the other predominates (e.g., see Murray and Hernstein, 1994). At the base, however, is a recognition that biology and culture are interdependent. Culture shapes biological processes through emotional expressions or cues and certain bodily functions like hunger. These are learned as a result of both the need for identity and group affiliation and the economic, political, and social (e.g., child-rearing, language, values) factors that influence what become acceptable ways of carrying out daily life. The result of learning one's culture leads to perceptible behaviors associated with an organized society. Such behavior is based on shared understandings which enable security, an ability to predict the behavior of others, and a knowledge of how to ensure survival.

Biologically based explanations for behavior, on the other hand, argue that many individual actions are tied to an unalterable inheritance. Such hereditary-difference explanations in the context of cultural relations are often termed "racist" because they argue that skin color or other physical characteristics signal certain behaviors or capacities like intelligence and emotional and psychological states. We will return to the issue of genetic explanations for I.Q. in chapter 5. As Thompson (1989) points out, biological theories assume that behaviors associated with particular ethnic and racial groups are inborn, heritable, and essentially unalterable. As with stereotypes associated with learned behavior, biologically based theories often are tied to sweeping generalizations and characterizations about the status and capabilities of members of identifiable groups. Feagin (1989) notes that such generalizations lead to conclusions that certain physical characteristics are linked in a causal way to psychological or intellectual charac-teristics and support a status hierarchy associated with superior and inferior racial groups. He explains such hierarchies as a response to the dominance displayed by certain groups as they subordinate and exploit others.

In the United States, "whites" and "nonwhites," including Asian Americans, African Americans, and Native Americans, constitute the significant racial divisions. Because membership in any one of these groups may automatically set one or more individuals off from European white populations, physical appearance is sometimes judged as equally racial and cultural. This is a recog-nition that an individual's skin color or other physical characteristics may be related to both high status and power or to ostracism or pariah status in a society. Thus, we believe that the interaction of an individual's ethnicity and race have individual and group consequences for shaping the relationships among groups and thus particular individual and group behaviors. We also recognize that there is often as much variation in behavior within the group that we label as there is between the members of that group and members of other groups.

Race and ethnic divisions are not always treated systematically through the use of labels. Petersen (1982), for example, notes that it is common in the United States to acknowledge ethnic divisions among whites but not among nonwhites. Thus, although Europeans are typically referred to by country of origin (e.g., Polish, Irish, Italian) and sometimes there is a distinction made among Asians (e.g., Japanese), reference in the United States to individuals from most other areas of the world are traditionally generic (e.g., Hispanics and Africans). He also notes, however, that Native Americans, although sometimes labeled as a whole, are enumerated by the United States government by their tribe of origin.

Social Class

Often entangled with ethnicity and race is *social class* (or *socioeconomic status*), another socially derived basis for labeling and explaining behavior and a third dimension along which societies are segmented. Social class reflects the level of political power and economic resources possessed or controlled by a race or ethnic group and is typically associated with years of formal education completed, the kinds of occupations typically pursued by a group, residential living patterns, and so on. Social class thus reflects the vertical dimension of such group segmentation. Its importance is noted as we attempt to make sense of the relationships among ethnic and racial groups and explain the ways in which resources are distributed. In some instances, identity within socioeconomic strata may be as strong as or stronger than that which binds members of particular ethnic and racial groups.

Socioeconomic or structural segments are best thought of as political or economic differences resulting in some groups having greater or lesser resources or status and hence power. The ethnic, racial, or socioeconomic groups—or a combination of such groups—which are dominant function to both preserve the controlling value system and to be the principal allocators of rewards in society (Schermerhorn, 1970). In the United States, it is primarily the white, historically European-based ethnic groups that constitute the middle and higher socio-economic populations. But such a characterization masks the many local relationships established among groups, none of whom might be white European in heritage. Nevertheless, nationwide it is most typical to find that those populations who are nonwhite and who are from non-European ethnic groups are those who predominate among the lower socioeconomic populations.

It should be noted that the definitions of ethnicity, race, and social class as well as the identities that individuals adopt based upon them are constantly changing, sometimes slowly and sometimes rapidly and dramatically. Some researchers have been asking how and why identities change and what accounts for that change. The question alone acknowledges that time and place determine to a large extent individual identities and that they can be changed without much effort. Being an "Asian," for example, is not limited, as it was in the recent past, to being a Chinese, Japanese, Korean, or Filipino. It now encompasses, among others, Cambodians, Vietnamese, Hmong, and Laotians. Similarly, being "Black" may include individuals whose physical appearance may be similar but whose background may link them with several very different geographical areas of the world. When ethnicity, race, and social class mix, there are more com-plexities. The Brazilian immigrant whose physical appearance is Black but whose profession is a medical doctor may be confronted with identifying as Latino, Brazilian, or Black, all intermingled with being associated with a member of the middle and upper socioeconomic strata. Individuals may seek to align themselves with whatever identity serves their individual or family aspirations, thereby broadening (e.g., Latino, South American) or narrowing (e.g., Brazilian, Medical Doctor) the basis on which the identity is fostered. The extent to which identities remain over generations is also an issue. White Americans of European descent, themselves the result of several cross-ethnic marriages, may chose to identify with one ethnic group in their background, but one to which they have little substantive connection.

Given the complexities identified above, it is no surprise that although the census provides the most complete picture of North America's racial and ethnic make up, that picture is a process and product contested by various groups, and its questions and system of classification change over time (Coughlin, 1993). In the 1990 census, Blacks are shown to constitute 12 percent of the U.S. population; Hispanics, 9 percent; Asian Americans, nearly 3 percent; and American Indians, Eskimo, and Aleuts, 0.8 percent. The proportion of non-Hispanic whites dropped from 83.5 percent in 1970 to 75.6 percent in 1990. The 1990 census provided seven new groups with which Asian Americans could identify themselves, found millions of Hispanics identifying themselves as members of an "other race" (probably based on a literal translation of the Spanish term *la raza*), and American Indians registered 700,000 more individuals than could be accounted for through birth and death records. Along with group pressure to reflect the needs of particular populations to satisfy their identification needs, the census provides an opportunity for people to match their sense of identity with the government's classification. The reasons this is important for people are many, but strong among them are the compensations, like affirmative action, minority contracting set-asides, and anti-discrimination laws, which parallel such identities.

These compensatory policies are among the reasons that the federal government is often pressured to review and potentially change the ways in which ethnic and racial groups are identified and statistics presented. Typically such pressures are intended to expand rather than reduce the number of categories. Arab Americans, for example, have expressed a desire to be identified as a separate category. Other groups wish to change their identification within existing categories. Some native Hawaiians, for example, express a desire to be moved from the Pacific Islander category to the American Indian category. Another issue is the growing number of individuals who are the offspring of mixed racial marriages (in the United States Black-white marriages quadrupled between 1985 and 1995) and who desire to reflect that mixture rather than being forced to chose among the composing elements. Some of these individuals desire a "multiracial" category. A question, here, however, is the impact such a new category would have on the current number of a single race being reported and whether parents or grandparents would constitute the defining feature. For example, Wheeler (1994) reports that a growing number of students—from 23 to 226 over a thirteen-year period—at the University of California, Berkeley, sought to enroll in a course he teaches entitled "People of Mixed Race Descent."

Acculturation and Assimilation

As groups interact in society they are influenced by one another. This influence may get translated into social change processes which can both blur or reduce as well as better define or enhance differences among and between them. Two common terms for these changes are *acculturation* and *assimilation*. Teske and Nelson (1974) analyze the concepts of acculturation and assimilation and conclude that they should be viewed as processes, not events, which involve two-way movements between and among individuals or groups. Acculturation and assimilation are separate processes, sometimes interrelated but not inter-dependent. Acculturation is the adoption of out-group values and is a necessary, though not sufficient, condition for assimilation. Acculturation depends on direct contact, is not necessarily egalitarian, and most often occurs in the direction of the dominant group. Acculturation need not depend on a positive orientation toward the out-group, and the out-group need not hold a positive orientation toward the acculturating group. Assimilation, on the other hand, is dependent on acculturation, requires both a positive orientation toward, and an identification with, the out-group on the part of the assimilating individual or group, and is contingent on acceptance by the out-group.

It is possible to find acculturation high but assimilation low. For example, some might argue that many African Americans in the United States find themselves in this position, having acculturated to the values of the dominant group but not having been accepted as being assimilable. It is also possible to find assimilation high and acculturation low. Thus, a visiting exchange student from another country might be accepted as an equal but he or she may not have accepted the dominant group's values. Finally, Teske and Nelson point to the individual who is accepted by the out-group, and who may be highly accul-turated in reference to the out-group, but fails to change his or her reference group. This condition appears to be applicable to most of those ethnic groups who have immigrated to the United States from Europe who have maintained allegiance to their originating ethnic groups. Thus, a Polynesian Hawaiian or a Hispanic from Latin America or the Caribbean, for example, may pass as acculturated members of the more dominant European group if certain behaviors become characteristic. They need not, however, become assimilated.

Acculturation and assimilation are important in placing certain behaviors, such as the language spoken, how one dresses, what food one eats, an individual's name, and so on, into some context. Each characteristic behavior may signal the extent to which an individual or group wishes to identify or has succeeded in identifying with a particular cultural population and is labeled a member of that population. It has been common among members of ethnic groups seeking to assimilate to the dominant white European population in the United States, for example, to avoid eating the foods or wearing the clothing associated with their cultural background or by speaking only English in the hope of creating greater out-group acceptance.

Glazer (1993) questions the viability of the concept of assimilation in the United States. He argues that the ideology of assimilation has been challenged primarily because of the lack of incorporation of African Americans, an outcome which he attributes to the discriminatory and prejudicial attitudes and behaviors toward them. Those groups which have been integrated into the political, educational, and economic institutions of society may be said to have assimilated themselves structurally. Simultaneously, however, these same groups may still maintain their ethnicity through primary relationships in their private lives. As Hraba (1979) notes, ethnicity is primarily an issue of identity and it will endure as long as it facilitates self-expression or it can be used in competition for scarce resources. He points to the 1960s in the United States as an era when subjective ethnic identities were rejuvenated and became a legitimate and proven means to make resource claims on behalf of interest groups. Education was a target for those special interests and played a major role in shaping relationships among groups as well as providing access to the resources which were being sought.

As groups seek to maintain their identity while also participating in the larger socioeconomic and political system, they must determine the ways to move back and forth in identity and behavior. Ogbu's studies of minority youngsters in schools (1987) found that some members of some groups, especially those who have come to the United States voluntarily, like the Japanese, Koreans, and Chinese, are able to adopt the values and identity of the larger society when it is necessary for school achievement, while also maintaining their ethnic identity with family and friends. He says that some members of minority groups whose immigration was not voluntary, like African Americans and Latinos, have a greater difficulty in adopting successful school behaviors because they equate such behavior with assimilation into the dominant group. Instead, they may actively resist achieving academically. There is also evidence (e.g., Mehan, Hubbard, and Villanueva, 1994), however, to indicate that students from these involuntary minority groups can be taught to develop skills which will enable them to succeed in school while simultaneously maintaining their cultural identity at home and in their neighborhood.

While in the 1990s we generally recognize that ethnic and racial groups will sometimes reinforce their identities and foster what might become boundaries around themselves—through religion, language, or daily behaviors—this was not always the case. Earlier in this century there was an expectation that groups would acculturate to the dominant group behaviors of the society, be assimilated by the dominant group, and thus contribute to a society that would blend all differences into a "melting pot." Part of this expectation was associated with the large numbers of immigrants who came from Europe to the United States prior to the turn of the century. Of the 5.25 million immigrants who arrived between the years 1881–1890, nearly 5 million came from Europe (U.S. Department of Justice, 1990). Robert Park (1950), a respected social scientist in the United States in the 1920s, was the proponent of the melting pot theory involving stages of inevitable assimilation of groups in society, a theory he applied not only to the United States but to the entire world. This melting pot view was generally accepted into the early 1960s. Petersen (1982) argues that it held credence because it was based primarily on political theory rather than on actual data and that assimilation was thought to be a one-way rather than a two-way process. Among others, the proposition failed to recognize the importance of the need of groups to preserve their heritages. It also underestimated the need to organize for community solidarity and to insure that group interests would be a way to leverage special recognition and services from various governmental agencies. The application of the "melting pot" theory has become even more problematic in recent years in the United States given the countries of origin of 7 million legal immigrants, most of whom came from Asia and Latin America, between 1981 and 1990 (U.S. Department of Justice, 1990).

Intergroup Relations: Economic, Political, and Social Dimensions

The ways in which groups interact in society are influenced by economic, political, and sociocultural factors. Gordon and Bhattacharyya (1992) argue, for example, that although the United States was founded on the basis of democratic principles which fostered the respect for diversity, such diversity has been accompanied by the dominance of those of European ancestry who have shaped the relations among and between groups. These two orientations toward diversity, one favoring heterogeneity with considerable autonomy and the other determined by dominant-group controls, have often been in conflict as particular groups have desired greater power or status at the expense of other groups or have threatened the stability, control, and interests of the dominant group. While the European heritage of dominance has survived in the United States, there have been many other, more localized relations among and between groups which have not involved white Europeans. In these instances, the groups involved have also established their relations based on economic, political, and social interests. In all instances, groups need to find ways to serve their interests while simultaneously taking actions which generally support the interests of the dominant group. Gordon and Bhattacharyya comment that such relationships center on questions of inclusiveness, representation, and social justice.

Feagin (1989) reviews various ways to explain racial and ethnic relations, including propositions based on social class, economic systems, and colonialism. Among the issues he highlights is that intergroup relations often depend on the extent to which members of one group believe that they gain economically, politically, or psychologically and thus see the need to protect social and economic privilege. White superiority over Blacks in the United States, for example, is cited by Feagin as an example of the expansion of European capitalism and the creation of a system of cheap slave labor and racial subordination. This system formed the basis for race prejudice and thus as a way to rationalize the exploitation of African Americans. He further notes that the role of the government has been important in defining and perpetuating the relations among and between groups. In the United States, for example, there have been restrictive immigration laws aimed at particular countries and ethnic groups and there has been the imprisonment of groups, like Japanese Americans in World War II. Further, the federal government has legislated the definitions of racial groups and interracial relationships, determined who would be eligible for citizenship, and favored the immigration of some groups over others.

Intergroup Relations: Economic Dimension

Examples of economic, political, and social pressures on shaping the relations among and between groups in this country can be traced to its origins. Bayor (1993) cites several instances where greater access to economic resources appears to dominate. In the 1680s, for example, one of the earliest conflicts occurred in New Amsterdam/New York between the Dutch and English as each vied for economic and political control. Dutch immigrants argued that the English dominance failed to provide opportunities for their success. Another example, this one from the early 1800s, involved numerous violent clashes in cities like Philadelphia, New York, and Boston between Irish immigrants and white native-born Protestants. These conflicts occurred over a variety of political, economic, religious, and educational issues and set the stage for long-term antagonisms. The riots of 1844 in Philadelphia, resulting in several days of violence and the burning of Roman Catholic churches were especially notable. The dominant Protestant groups saw in the Irish a threat to job security and traditional values propagated through an alien and challenging Catholic religious movement. Also in the 1800s, Bayor cites the threat to the lower-class Irish posed by African Americans in New York, which led to numerous assaults against African Americans. One of these was the 1863 riots in which Black-Irish friction over jobs and neighborhoods led to Irish gangs attacking African Americans in New York. The Irish perceived the abolition of slavery along with the general intolerance of Catholicism in the larger society as threats to their economic status and cultural survival.

Two final examples from Bayor show how economic influences shape intergroup conflict. The immigration of Chinese to California in the 1860s and later was feared because of the likelihood that they would work for cheaper wages in jobs held by white immigrant groups. The Chinese were viewed as competitors for jobs and strike breakers, as well as a threat to racial homogeneity. Anti-Chinese legislation in California called for an investigation into the effects of Chinese immigration as violence between groups occurred throughout numerous cities in the West. The other economic example from Bayor involves immigrants from Cuba and their challenge to Blacks in Miami in the 1960s. Following the Cuban Revolution and the large influx of Cubans to Miami, Blacks found increased economic competition and perceived favoritism from the federal government for Cubans and other Latin American immigrants. The changes in the political and economic structure in Miami fueled the race riots of 1968 and the continued resentment among groups.

Intergroup Relations: Political Dimension

Beyond primarily economic bases for establishing relations between and among groups, political concerns have often dominated such interaction. Simon (1993) cites public opinion polls taken in the United States during the past fifty years to establish the premise that, contrary to the image presented in the society of an open door for immigrants, the population at any given time has continuously viewed newcomers with suspicion, distrust, and hostility. This generally negative attitude toward immigrants, argues Simon, has established the numerous political efforts to limit immigration. She notes, for example, that in the Colonial era, all of the New England colonies except Rhode Island excluded non-Puritans. Beginning in the 1660s, naturalization acts were passed limiting citizenship to foreign-born Protestants. During subsequent years all colonies passed laws against Jews and Catholics holding offices and voting. She cites the Chinese Exclusion Act of 1882 as a demonstration of racist behavior by Congress, as it suspended the entry of Chinese workers and limited U.S. citizenship to those Chinese born in the United States. This exclusion was extended to the Japanese after the turn of the century through other means and was symptomatic of the general anti-Asian sentiment throughout the country. The racial exclusion of Chinese was not lifted until 1943.

The history of negative attitudes and values held by a majority of the population toward minority group immigrants in the United States appears common. Simon reports that during the period 1946–1990, respondents to various opinion surveys favored a decrease in the number of immigrants permitted to enter the country. She notes that at no point in this 45-year period did more than 13 percent of the population believe that immigration should exceed that permitted by law. This generally negative view of immigrants appears likely to be carried into the twenty-first century. A recent *Time* magazine survey (Nelan, 1993), for example, reported a continuing negative perception toward immigrants. Some 73 percent of a national sample favored strictly limiting immigration, up from 67 percent in 1985. A majority, 60 percent, also favored changes in federal law to reduce the number of immigrants who enter the United States legally. Such widely held opinions provide a basis for continued political intervention in the immigration arena. An example in 1993 and 1994 involved limiting Haitian immigration to the United States following government changes there.

The generally negative views toward immigrants have been manifested in other ways in the history of the country. In 1917, for example, the U.S. Congress mandated that a literacy test be administered as a means to limit the number of immigrants from Italy and the Slavic East, where the education levels achieved by the populations were low. Thus, it was expected that fewer immigrants from these areas would pass such a test of English and be able to migrate to the United States. Additionally, in 1921, and again in 1924, quota laws were passed which established the annual number of entrants into the United States based on nationality. The 1921 law was aimed at limiting immigrants from southern and eastern Europe, as they were deemed unable to assimilate to the existing population in the United States and were seen biologically inferior to the Nordic stock from western and northern Europe (Hraba, 1979). Other pieces of legislation during the first two decades of the twentieth century limited groups on the basis of, among others, political activities and ideologies. Fuchs (1993) notes that more recently, in 1980, 1986, and 1990, Congress and the executive branches of government have enacted policies which dramatically increased immigration, especially from Latin America and Asia. He argues that this has caused an increasing backlash against immigrants. Furthermore, he notes, neither branch of the federal government has given much attention to the implications of such actions for ethnic policies involving language and affirmative action.

Intergroup Relations: Social Dimension

Associated with the primarily economic and political influences shaping intergroup relations are sociocultural influences. Purposely increasing contact between members of ethnic groups, for example, has been a value held by many social planners as a means to achieve societal harmony and greater integration. But studies often find that contact alone between groups does not necessarily result in improved intergroup relations. Schools and the workplace may be integrated across ethnic groups, for example, but neighborhood and voluntary organizations like clubs, churches, business establishments, and recreational areas of the neighborhood are often demarcated by ethnic boundaries. Language usage, food, dress, and similar group identification characteristics serve to reinforce such boundaries. In studying contact among and between groups, Allport (1954) concluded that for contact to result in positive outcomes, participants must be of roughly equal status and be pursuing similar goals in a cooperative manner, and the relationships must be sanctioned in law and by the government.

These conditions are obviously not being achieved among many segments in the population of the United States. The National Conference of Christians and Jews (1993) conducted a poll to assess the relationships among and between ethnic and racial groups. They found that African Americans, Latino Americans, and Asian Americans generally believed that white Americans (1) are insensitive to other people and have a long history of bigotry and prejudice; (2) believe they are superior and can boss other people around; and (3) control power and wealth and do not want to share it with nonwhites. Some 80 percent of African Americans, 60 percent of Latin Americans, and 57 percent of Asian Americans were reported to have felt that they lack the same opportunities enjoyed by whites. The report notes that the members of the minority groups hold very negative stereotypes about members of other minority groups. While such negative perceptions are common, the poll results indicated that there is also considerable positive contact between and among groups. Whites, for example, often report having good friends among members of the minority groups.

Even though ethnic groups may maintain distance in certain aspects of their lives while sustaining regular contact in other aspects, there is pressure for socio-cultural actions to be tied to the manner in which daily life becomes reflective of the interests of the dominant political and economic sectors of society. Antonio Gramsci (see Broccoli, 1977), writing in the 1920s, was one of the earliest commentators to point to the ideological function of the state, arguing that the dominant group uses institutions to shape the values and beliefs of the society in directions compatible with those of the dominant group and thereby influences the ways in which people think about themselves and their relations to others and to the state. Complementing this view is the work of Raymond Williams (1961), whose study of the history of education in Great Britain argues that school curricula reflect deliberate choices made by competing power groups to enhance their social power and control. Similarly, Pierre Bourdieu (1973) points to the different kinds of knowledge that are available to ethnic, racial, and socioeconomic groups in society. Elite knowledge and culture, he argues, is unequally distributed through schools and thus serves to maintain or increases the economic, political, and social gaps between and among groups. To combat this hegemony, according to Gramsci, necessitates the development of a counter-force, an alternative set of values and beliefs based in the working class. Such a political force, argued Gramsci, would ultimately lead to substituting itself for those who currently hold power.

Implied in Gramsci's view of the state as an instrument of the dominant capitalist class is a socialization process which pulls toward one common set of standards—typically national—as opposed to pulling toward pluralism and diversity. This view constitutes one aspect of an approach to intergroup relations proposed by Schermerhorn (1970), who believes that groups are integrated in a society in accord with the on-going activities and objectives of the dominant group in that society. This occurs either through a tendency toward common, society-wide lifestyles and institutional participation or through attempts by separate groups to retain and preserve unique cultural attributes as well as to seek greater autonomy politically and economically. If the tendencies are in opposition—one desiring closer relations while another seeks greater autonomy, for example—the integration process is likely to be conflictual. Thus, one has to look to the congruence or difference of aims to understand how integration as a dynamic, continuous, and never-ending process is likely to move.

Education and Intergroup Relations: Economic, Political, and Social Dimensions

Educational institutions may well be the most central and important institutions in understanding intergroup relations. Schooling is society's way of telling all of its own members, as well as those in other societies, what is of most importance to pass on to the new generation. And because at the primary and secondary levels, schools constitute the only institution that is characterized by compulsory attendance, and at the higher levels, the primary gateway to income and status, they fit well into an analysis of group values, identities, and goals. Educational institutions take on special importance across ethnic, racial, and socioeconomic groups in the United States because civil rights policies are based on access to resources. Schools figure prominently under such policies because they are the institutional means for achieving status and resources. Hein (1993) establishes the basis for this point as he compares the United States' intergroup relations policies with those found in France. He notes, for example, that while both societies ban discrimination on the basis of race, religion, and national origin, they differ in their implementation of this policy. In France, for example, there are no policies to promote hiring for diversity (e.g., affirmative action) or to redistrict voting along racial and ethnic lines. But French policies reach out to impose more severe penalties on racial and ethnic insults. Thus, Hein makes the point that French policy seeks to guarantee minorities' rights to membership, such as protection against hate speech. In the United States, on the other hand, emphasis is placed on gaining access to resources and compensating for past injustices (e.g., affirmative action), among others, all of which Hein argues tends to increase the conflict among and between groups as each vies for income, status, and power. Hein argues that the United States' policy fails to provide a model for how race and ethnic relations ought to be conducted and instead makes minorities the agent of change. Thus, in the United States, because schools act as the guardians of credentials and diplomas needed for jobs, they take on added importance.

By knowing that all individuals and groups in a given society must be integrated in some articulated and functional way for the society to perpetuate itself, it is possible to assess the role of schooling and other institutions in shaping the integration process. Schools are especially visible in this regard, as they are society's sorting and recruiting institutions. They sort and recruit through grades, diplomas, and other credentials which are said to represent the achievement or lack of achievement of the individuals who participate. In this way, schools are gatekeepers. They constitute arenas for testing the extent to which groups are satisfied or dissatisfied with patterns of participation. More specifically, they test the acceptance of predominant ideologies and cultural values which either support the status quo or facilitate change and thus greater subordinate-group access to the socioeconomic rewards of society. The basic choice of the subordinate group, which again may be represented by a single or combined ethnic, racial, and/or structural segment, is to challenge the dominant group to create interaction or remain inactive and immobile and thereby protect the accepted and patterned behavior which accompanies the status quo. The dominant population must see that the subordinates continue to be motivated to play their roles in society by facilitating consensus or exerting power. Sometimes the conflict which results from pursuing consensus or using power can result in new levels of integration. At other times, it can result in violence, revolution, and a massive upheaval in the structure of society.

Schools reflect this dynamic interplay among and between groups. To some, schools function to incorporate all social groups on a roughly equal basis, while to others schools are seen as perpetuating cultural and structural divisions and thus are said to sort and recruit individuals into society in an unequal and stratified way. In the first view, school access and promotion are assumed to be acquired by those who are most intelligent and skillful without regard to their social or cultural characteristics (Harbison, 1973; Foster, 1977). The opposing argument says that schools reinforce social distinctions by placating those from subordinate groups and gaining their compliance without changing their position in society (Cohen,

1975; Carnoy 1976). Ogbu (1978), for example, argues that dominant groups provide inferior schooling to caste-like racial and ethnic minorities in the United States and limit their access to the rewards of schooling in later life. La Belle and White (1979) reflect on these opposing views and note that it is important to look at both cultural and structural interactions in school as they may differ in their intent and impact. Thus, bilingual education, vocational training, or separate school facilities may well have very different implications according to the particular relationships among ethnic, racial, or socioeconomic groups. Hence, fostering mother-tongue instruction at the elementary level, an acknowledgment of diversity and the needs of particular ethnic groups, might be accompanied by other centrally determined criteria like the need to secure a high standardized college admissions test score in English, in order to proceed through the educational system, thereby maintaining ultimate control in the hands of the dominant group.

The extent to which the dominant group facilitates host-language instruction or other local initiatives is interactive with the way it ensures the legitimacy of the nation-state. The legitimacy of a nation depends in the long run on the ability of its leadership to meet the needs and interests of the population. Thus, there must be opportunities available for individuals to achieve their needs and the needs of other members in the society. At the same time, the population must internalize certain attachments to national symbols and obedience to the state's authority. The extent to which the nation permits diversity to compete with national or dominant-group interests constitutes a type of balancing act carried out in schools. This balancing weighs the interests of the dominant group and the subordinate groups as each vies to influence the ways in which the schooling process is conducted and on what the process is designed to achieve.

Some argue that the relationship between the dominant group, the state, and education is an interaction tied to the nature of the economy. Carnoy (1992), for example, identifies two opposing views of the state and its relationships to educational organizations and processes, both of which are derived from the state's larger association with economic relations. One sees the state as independent of the larger society and thus intervening inappropriately in the activities of the economy and society, while the other sees the state as reflecting and reinforcing economic relations and thus the dominant-subordinate group relations which characterize the society. These views are not dissimilar to the effects of education discussed above. In other words, if the state is viewed as independent of the society and economy, individuals are left alone to make it through the educational system on the basis of their own abilities. If, on the other hand, the state is viewed as a necessary player in ensuring the equal opportunity of members of the society and education is deemed an important avenue of mobility, then the state must intervene to correct inequalities which result from the lack of controls associated with free-market economies.

Beyond the reflection of economic relations, schools also are the center of political activity. Aguirre and Martinez (1993), for example, argue that for Chicanos, the issue of low achievement in school did not receive much attention until the 1960s. In 1968, the authors note, thousands of Mexican American students walked out of schools in protest to what they perceived as discrimination against them. The protesters cited the prohibition of the use of Spanish in school, the overrepresentation of Mexican American students in classes for the educable mentally retarded, the lack of English language courses for Spanish speakers, and the lack of courses of study in the curricula on Mexican Americans. These issues in the 1970s ultimately led to the development of government-sponsored bilingual education programs, new guidelines for the placement of students in EMR classes, and to affirmative action programs as a means to undo past wrongs. In higher education, Aguirre and Martinez note, affirmative action policies established nationally led to special admissions programs through which race and ethnicity could be taken into account in making admissions decisions.

There are many examples of political influences in education through the state intervening in educational matters—from the language to be used for instruction to the theories to explain the origin of life, the fiction and nonfiction books that should be on the library shelves, and the segregation and desegregation of schools. But these intrusions are the more noticeable ways that interventions have impact. There are also many less noticeable and more subtle ways that the dominant group and the state seek to control schools and prevent racial and ethnic groups and other religious, political, and special interest groups from exerting too much influence on the schooling process. Schools are often at the center of these interests because what goes on inside them is assumed to have an influence on what students learn as they grow up. Thus, interest groups, including the family and community, wish to establish the values and behaviors which act as a prototype for an adult style of life. The dominant group and the state wish to do the same, but based on nonfamilial and universalistic considerations, such that the individual going through the school system is molded to serve the aims of the social system.

Yehudi Cohen (1971) notes this tension between the universalistic values, criteria, and standards of performance sought by the state as a means to ensure its long-term viability and those of separate interest groups. He argues that one of the goals of the state is to subvert local—especially kin—sources of solidarity, loyalty, and authority. It does this by establishing an ideology—if not a reality—of uniformity among the members of the society. Through schools as a major means of accomplishing this uniformity, standardized sets of symbols to which all members of the society can be trained to respond uniformly are established. Uniform dress codes, the language spoken in school, the books which are read, the paraphernalia that gets displayed in schools, the culture heroes who are praised, and so on are all ways that Cohen sees the schools helping to inculcate a uniform set of ideological symbols. The goal of the state is thus to have the schools serve the economic and political structures through preparing individuals to behave in one correct way, rather than to foster the life of free inquiry.

As special interest groups tied to race, ethnicity, and socioeconomic status gain greater power and status in society, they seek to use the schools to push an agenda which reflects their particular values and prototypic behaviors. They also seek to use the schools as a means for their long-term viability, not only through what goes into the curriculum—or the experiences that a learner has under the direction and sponsorship of the educational institution—but how the curriculum facilitates their access to the resources of the wider society. Because the curriculum is so broad a concept, there is often a concentrated effort to focus on what books are on reading lists or in libraries. It is for this reason that those who wish to change the curriculum, especially the textbooks, are confronted by what James Banks (1993) calls the "western traditionalists," those who defend a curriculum dominated by such European writers as Milton, Dante, and Shakespeare. He argues that such defenders are confronting both those who wish to infuse the curriculum with ethnic-specific as well as multicultural content. Because of the attention drawn to these conflicts in the late 1980s and 1990s, more attention has been directed to the textbooks that students are asked to read as a part of their formal studies.

Textbooks as a Reflection of Group Interests

As suggested above, of all the formal education issues which draw public interest and scrutiny, the textbooks assigned to students as part of their coursework probably rank among the most visible. School texts are typically reviewed for adoption at various levels of the formal school bureaucracy, from the teacher in the classroom and the local school board to the state superintendent of instruction and the state board of education. Parents see school texts as their sons and daughters bring them home for study, and interest groups, from religious organizations to environmentalists, scrutinize them for the value positions they take on topics of interest. Because they constitute such a large part of the publishing industry, authors and publishers of school texts are often major players in the adoptions process. It is common, for example, for such authors and publishers to tailor the substance of textbooks to a state, a city, or even a single district.

Throughout the process of school textbook adoption, the potential texts are reviewed to determine the extent to which they distort or hide assumptions, omit facts, or make subtle distinctions and emphases and thus represent particular group interests as a means to shaping attitudes and behaviors in support of certain groups. This kind of analysis in recent decades has also been done by scholars. Anyon (1977), for example, studied secondary school history texts, concluding that a variety of arguments in the texts, although presented in an unbiased way, serve to provide ideological justification for the interests of the wealthy and powerful. The symbolic legitimating of such groups through the curricula becomes a means of soliciting the support of the lower classes for an economic and social system which has not served them well. In another study, Fitzgerald (1980) found that textbook bias was longstanding in U.S. schools. Prior to the 1930s, for example, he found that texts gave little attention to immigrants other than the challenge they posed for long-term assimilation. The texts failed to describe immigrant lifestyles, work, or motivations for immigrating. Fitzgerald (1980) notes that it was not until well into the 1960s that the immigrants were actually described as a distinct segment of the population and the concept of a multicultural society took hold. Involuntary immigrants, especially African Americans before this same period of the 1960s, were typically described in degrading ways that would justify the power of whites.

Fitzgerald's study of history textbooks used in the schools notes that while the 1960s provided a dramatic reversal in the country away from ethnic bias, a different path was followed with textbook treatment of American Indians. In that case, they were accorded considerable respect and importance through much of the nineteenth century as texts provided detailed descriptions of tribal differences and leadership descriptions. As the century drew to a close, however, Indians were being described as "savage" "barbarous," and "half-civilized". "Childlike," "lazy," and "cruel" were the terms used in the 1920s. In the 1930s and 1940s, Fitzgerald indicates that only elementary school–level texts mentioned Indians, and by the 1950s they were hardly mentioned at all. She attributes this change in Native American treatment to the textbook writers and the changing nature of the society. She says that in the early nineteenth century the Indians were viewed as an object of national pride. As their locus moved west, however, and the textbook writers remained in the East, there was a growing indifference to their condition and they were characterized based on their earlier threats to settlers in the West.

It was in the late 1960s, however, that major changes were noted in the textbook treatment of most of the minority groups that lived in the United States. The cause of such change can be found in the protests registered by the minority ethnic groups themselves. In Detroit, for example, the local branch of the NAACP (National Association for the Advancement of Colored People) charged that one textbook depicted slavery in a positive way and called on the school board to withdraw it from its classrooms. The book was withdrawn and the effect across the country was to unleash similar actions in other cities and by other groups which felt that certain books were abusive and biased. The general tenor in the country at the time was that all texts had portrayed the United States as a white, middle-class society rather than as multicultural and multiracial. As the civil rights movement gained momentum in the 1960s, and pressure for desegregation in schools, the workplace, and housing increased, the textbook issue was one more to which attention was drawn.

One of the most recent movements concerned with what students are reading in school is associated with politically conservative religious organizations. Among them, the Christian Coalition, along with other organizations such as the Family Research Council and Focus on the Family, is characteristic of those who have declared opposition to school curricula which mention homosexuality, abortion, separation of church and state, and women's rights. They favor the teaching of religion in school and school prayer. DelFattore (1992) argues that it is this far-right conservative movement which is responsible for the sharp increase in school textbook protests in the 1980s and 1990s. The religious right is concerned with the swing away from books which present traditional family, religious, and patriotic themes to those which endorse multiculturalism, environmentalism, and globalism.

These and other advocates of particular values and interests which attempt to shape the experiences that students have under the direction of the school are part of the tension which puts group interests at the forefront of educational issues. DelFatore argues that they reflect the conflict between centralization—the drive for a national curriculum—and the lobbying of special interest groups for greater local control through the publication of specially created textbooks for a community's schools. Whether the local group represents, among others, a religious view, an ethnic view, or a political view, it is simply reflecting the battleground over the school curricula as a means to influence the socialization of students and the achievement of a particular vision of society's future.

These conflicts over the curriculum, while taking place in and reflecting the larger societal context, ultimately take place inside of schools, where federal, state, and local policies are implemented through the various interest groups that constitute the school population. Much of the pressure on school policy, therefore, emerges from legal and political decisions and the power that is held by the various social actors who have an interest in educational decision making. The source of power is in the influence or resource that the individual or group has that is deemed important for the institution to carry out its mission. Within the school, there exists another set of individuals and groups who also act to influence the day-to-day activities which affect the people who function within it. These individuals are divided into interests, subunits, and subcultures who participate, through bargaining and compromise, in the day-to-day operation of the institution. It is within this outside and inside set of relationships that the activities for students are planned and implemented.

Conclusion

We will return periodically in the remaining chapters to the issue of who controls educational curricula and how that control relates to segmentation in the wider society. As the pages of this chapter indicate, that relationship is complex and ever changing as labels and behavior associated with ethnicity, race, and social class take on both technical and popular meanings. Further, as the composition and status of the segments reflected in these concepts are altered, different relations occur between and among groups. Such changes are especially apparent in schools at all levels.

Ethnicity, race, and social class, or the concepts used to better comprehend intergroup relations, serve as heuristic devices to organize information and assist in explaining the nature and direction of such relations. Although sometimes used in stereotypic fashion, with care such terms can both acknowledge variation as well as point to the use of culture as an important tool for needs assessment and program planning and implementation. Thus, such concepts have direct relevance to those who have an interest in multicultural and ethnic studies efforts.

The relevance of the application of ethnicity, race, and social class to educational settings is seen in linking intergroup relations to economic, political, and social influences; acculturation and assimilation or one- and two-way change processes involving both subordinate and dominant groups; teaching, learning, and assessment in determining readiness and accomplishment; furthering insights into the relationships between environmental and biological bases of behavior; and the extent to which subordinate-group autonomy will be permitted to exist in the context of dominant-group expectations and controls. Such dynamics will be explored in the next two chapters as we further chronicle the emergence of multiculturalism and then turn to the development and status of ethnic studies.

Part 2

*Multiculturalism and Ethnic Studies:
A Contemporary View*

CHAPTER 3

The Rise of Multiculturalism

While ethnic and other group-specific studies dominated much of the movement toward diversity in higher education in the 1960s and 1970s, in the 1980s a new phenomena appeared: multiculturalism. In this chapter, we review definitions of multiculturalism, summarize views of its critics and supporters, and examine its historical antecedents in American higher education. After presenting examples of recently instituted multicultural requirements, we suggest how some now see multiculturalism as a possible threat to ethnic studies.

Over the last decade, *multiculturalism* has taken on a number of meanings. At elementary or secondary levels where the approach is often centered on a specified curriculum ("multicultural education"), multiculturalism has had a variety of goals. Some programs emphasize teaching the culturally different in order to transition students from various groups into the mainstream. Other programs focus on helping students from different ethnic groups get along better or on teaching about specific groups to promote pluralism. Still other programs actively seek to promote cultural pluralism and social equality, while the most progressive efforts seek to prepare students to promote cultural diversity and to challenge structural inequality (Sleeter and Grant, 1987).

In colleges and universities in the United States, multiculturalism has generally not taken the form of a single course or curriculum. Rather, multiculturalism has served as a cover term for developments, movements, and points of view related to growing diversity, to an assumption that students will be employed in increasingly diverse environments, and to critiques of societal and educational power relations. While many of the issues relate to study and research, they also encompass aspects of campus life such as the amount of weight that school regulations should give to individual rights for free speech versus the weight they should give to group rights for protection from stereotyping and abuse.

Among the assumptions in recent literature by proponents of multiculturalism in higher education are the following (Nieto, 1993):

• The curriculum needs to reflect the dramatic demographic, social, and economic changes in U.S. society.

- Pedagogy must change to engage students more in their own learning and to promote critical thinking.
- A multicultural perspective should not just be confined to the social sciences and humanities, but should permeate the entire curriculum, pedagogy, and education structure.
- Future teachers need to be prepared to teach students of widely different cultures, languages, and experiences.

Multiculturalism has been associated with controversy. In the late 1980s conservatives attacked those who challenged the existing higher education curriculum by labeling their multicultural efforts as politically inspired. At the heart of the resulting "political correctness" debate has been the question of whether higher education should teach a curriculum based on the traditionally taught Western literature, values, and history, or whether more diverse perspectives should be taught, particularly those deemed important by subordinate groups, including racial and ethnic minorities, women, and gays and lesbians. The controversy has moved beyond academia with the popular press weighing in for and against multiculturalism. Some commentators have offered sweeping criticisms of multiculturalism as a divisive menace to society (Bernstein, 1994).

In addition to the jabs about "political correctness," critics of multiculturalism raise more substantial problems with the concept and its many manifestations. A common concern is that a new, broader multicultural canon may fail to give students from across the country a common intellectual community and contribute to a lack of unity in their learning. Another concern is that faculty who promote multicultural ideas for introductory courses are, in fact, simply bringing in the fashionable ideologies that preoccupy their own narrow scholarship, seminars, and conferences. Critics have also charged that those who would change the curriculum have a political agenda (Kimball, 1990). Others have argued that the traditional canon does not necessarily represent a conservative point of view; many of the writers included in the traditional canon were rebels and radicals to their own societies.

The debate about multiculturalism raises a number of important questions about higher education in a pluralistic, liberal democracy. A basic issue facing colleges and universities is whether teaching and research should focus on particular groups or on the pluralistic nature of American society. Diane Ravitch (1990) maintains that a "pluralistic" multiculturalism has become an organizing principal of American society. Because of the widespread acceptance of this principal, young people today learn that cultural diversity is positive. However, Ravitch warns that ethnic interest groups have begun to politicize the curriculum. Advocates of what she labels "particularistic" multiculturalism declare that biology controls a person's culture and that teaching specific multicultural models will raise students' self-esteem and academic performance. Particularistic multiculturalism, she says, rejects interactions between groups that might blur distinctions between them. She characterizes multiculturalism as a political movement that advocates a kind of cultural predestination. The movement's specific proposals for change in the curriculum are primarily weapons to criticize existing universities, educational systems, and disciplines.

A second question is whether multiculturalism is about cultural diversity or whether it is really about basic political divisions in society and higher education. One interpretation of the latter position links multiculturalism closely to leftist politics and traces its roots to the 1960s. In that era, students wanted the curriculum to reflect the wider needs in society, demanded relevance in courses, and wanted courses to be taught with political commitment, rather than with dispassionate academic distance. Ethnic studies, women's studies, and courses in clinical legal education arose as part of this move toward relevance (Getman, 1992).

The more conservative late 1970s and 1980s brought less emphasis on this kind of change, but the basic curriculum and pedagogical issues continued. Over the last decade two polar positions have developed. One group calls for academic objectivity, such that the students of a political science professor shouldn't be able to guess her or his political party affiliation. The other group value scholars who are more open about their personal political beliefs and bring their view into the classroom. The multiculturalists are part of this latter group. In the 1990s, Getman says, the calls for multiculturalism replaced the call for relevance. Multiculturalism's proponents tend to be professors on the political left who came of age in the 1960s and who find political engagement stimulating.

The highly visible controversy over multiculturalism has tended to obscure the fact that the impact of multiculturalism on many students has been quite limited. Courses on topics related to race and ethnicity, feminist studies, gay and lesbian studies, and other group studies are fairly peripheral to most students' course of study and have even less to do with their day-to-day lives in a college or university. Concentrated in upper-division or graduate courses, often in their own departments or institutes, with limited enrollment, multiculturalism has little effect on most students. Even many critics of multiculturalism agree that its impact is limited to courses in Western civilization—courses in literature, philosophy, history, and the social sciences (Douglas, 1992).

Multiculturalism has generated the most intense debate when changes are suggested in core requirements (such as in first-year composition or literature courses), courses on diversity are required, or changes are made to institutional regulations (such as what students may or may not post on campus computer bulletin boards). Although the core curriculum has remained fairly traditional and largely based on Western European culture, advocates of multiculturalism and their predecessors have been engaged in major efforts to bring more diversity to college and university campuses since the 1940s.

Early Multicultural Education Efforts

Multiculturalism generally came later to college campuses (1980s) than it did to elementary and secondary schools (1970s). However, multicultural efforts at both levels of institutions have built on earlier attempts to use higher education and the social sciences to understand and promote pluralism. In the 1940s and early 1950s the intercultural (later "intergroup") education movement was associated with higher education through teacher training programs, action research, and utilization of the knowledge generated by universities' expanding social science departments.

Intercultural education began as a community movement backed by mainstream liberal religious groups and fueled by the rise of fascism and the concern that emerged during World War II that the United States live up to its stated ideals of democracy and human rights. The movement drew on a cultural pluralism approach to intergroup relations that encouraged cultural pride and promoted tolerance for ethnic and cultural differences. The movement's advocates sought to understand the nature of prejudice and to find effective means to change prejudicial attitudes and stereotypes (Glazer, 1977). The movement focused on the individual relationships rather than on group political or economic power. Democratic human relations and full rights for minorities were several of its important values (Cook, 1947).

Advocates of intercultural education saw the problem of intergroup relations as one that higher education could and should address. They believed colleges and universities were ideal places to enlighten students to the problems of prejudice. Higher education could also provide the tools to attack prejudice in the community through utilization of the techniques of psychology, sociology, and anthropology. Moreover, advocates saw higher education faculty as a source of ideas about intergroup education and accepted that the community was a laboratory for intergroup research.

By the mid-1940s, educational journals were beginning to carry articles on intercultural education. Within a few years intercultural education had moved more fully into universities and teacher-training institutions, with national organizations completing and publishing major studies. At the same time, the movement came to be referred to more frequently by the term *intergroup education*.

A major effort in the introduction of intergroup education into the nation's colleges and universities was the College Study in Intergroup Relations. From 1945 to 1949 the American Council on Education's Council on Cooperation in Teacher Education carried out this effort to improve future teachers' preparation in intergroup education. The project, funded by the National Conference on Christians and Jews, was based on the following assumptions:

- That intergroup relations were of supreme importance to educators, particularly to teacher educators
- That intergroup tensions would increase in the United States as time passed after World War II
- That the resolution of intergroup tensions was the greatest test of a democracy (Cook, 1950)

Twenty-four teacher-education institutions were selected for participation from the many that applied. While the twenty-four represented a range of institutions, there were none from the West Coast (for financial reasons), nor were there any Catholic universities (none applied). Among those represented were several historically Black colleges and some institutions that were segregated or maintained segregated student housing. The study's general conclusions included the following:

- Intergroup problems are most evident in race, creed, immigrant cultures, socioeconomic levels, and rural-urban heritage.
- The primary reasons for institutional inaction are teacher insecurity, administrative unconcern, and community pressure.
- The college study was able to facilitate change at small institutions but not at large ones.
- The attitudes of future teachers—who are products of their culture—change, but very little, as a result of education.
- Indirect approaches with student participation appear to be a better way to democratize student behaviors than do direct approaches.
- Campus and student culture can be changed through group work in which students take the initiative.
- Change in intergroup education cannot come from administrative order, but must be self motivated. (Cook, 1950)

In light of the controversies over multiculturalism in higher education in the 1990s, several of these conclusions are of particular interest. First, the study's finding that group problems—we would say "conflicts"—are based in social class as well as racial and ethnic divisions reflects a continuing concern. Less important seems to be the finding that students can be divided into those from rural and those from urban areas. The growth of mass media and the expansion of consumer and youth cultures have most likely reduced the rural-urban gap among college students. The study's findings, which showed that institutional cultures and related attitudes are slow to change and are particularly resistant to changes initiated from the outside, also relate to current diversity efforts. In chapters 5 and 6 we shall see how change is often guided by dominant groups.

In the early 1950s, another study examined intergroup education in the nation's liberal arts colleges and universities (Smiley, 1952). The report on the study raised a number of issues and trends. First, the study documented how intergroup education was broadening in scope and definition. From the 1940s, intergroup education's primary concern had been for improving relations among ethnic, racial, religious, and social groups in society. However, Smiley described a field that included diverse elements such as international relations, area studies (Far Eastern studies, for example), interreligious programs, courses on race relations, and courses on specific groups such as African Americans. By the 1950s it was clear that the intergroup education field did not have one definition. Secondary education and teachers' colleges tended to identify intergroup education with relations between majority and minority groups in the United States. In liberal arts colleges the definition of intergroup education was broader and, for some, included the relations of capital and labor, and even the relations within families.

Second, the study demonstrated that intergroup education's advocates were promoting not just a change in curriculum but a change in campus climate. The formal definition of intergroup education used in the study of liberal arts colleges was "the entire range of the college's endeavor to educate students for democratic intergroup relations—not only the formal instructional program but also the whole social climate and institutional pattern of the college: extra-curricular activities, admissions, appointments, and housing" (Smiley, p. 11).

Third, the study emphasized intergroup education as spanning the curriculum with less emphasis than in previous years on courses about specific groups. Intergroup education was multidisciplinary and spanned the life of the institution. Smiley found that fewer group courses were being offered, suggesting that as the field grew there was less emphasis on studies of separate group cultures. However, more courses were being offered in sociology and anthropology. At the same time, intergroup education also emphasized the contribution of aspects of college life other than the academic, including personnel policies and administrators.

Fourth, the study highlighted the gap between the ideal of what higher education said it wanted and what was implemented in practice. The study showed that nearly all the institutions and administrators who applied endorsed the value of diversity and believed a diverse institution added to student learning. However, this general endorsement of intergroup education was not backed by concrete commitments. Few of these institutions and administrators reported requiring core courses in intergroup education or related areas.

Finally, the questions raised by the study and related commentary are similar to some asked today. The questions facing the field included the following:

- Should programs aim at the development of a unified national (global) culture or the fostering of cultural diversity?
- Should education be primarily concerned with equalizing the opportunities for individuals or with relationships between groups?
- Should intergroup education constitute a field in itself or should it be one aspect of the study of human relations?
- Should college organizations better serve intergroup relations by being blind to differences or by directly addressing them through interfaith fellowships, interracial associations, and the like?

The intercultural/intergroup education movement faded into human relations courses and other individually oriented approaches to prejudice and racism. What remains striking, given the surge of protest in the 1960s, is how the movement ignored group power and how it lacked voices from subordinate communities or individuals. However, the movement did leave a legacy that included a broad definition of intergroup relations to include social class as well as race and ethnicity, an acknowledgement of the importance of what is now known as "campus climate" for intergroup relations, an appreciation of the complexities of bringing about change in group relations in higher education, and an understanding that the study of intergroup relations spans the curriculum.

Themes in the Multiculturalism Debate

Advocates of multiculturalism emphasize a number of themes in their prescription for change in higher education. The first of these themes is that the curriculum should reflect the increasing diversity of American society and its higher education institutions by race, ethnicity, gender, age, sexual orientation, and physical ability.

The argument says that despite some setbacks in the 1980s for African Americans, particularly for African American males, access to higher education has increased in the United States over the past fifty years. In particular, over the last several decades more African Americans, Native Americans, Asian Americans, and Hispanics have enrolled in colleges and universities. More women and more older persons are attending higher education. In many urban areas on the East and West Coasts, significant numbers of recently arrived immigrants are enrolled, particularly in community colleges. Persons who are physically challenged are more able to attend. To cite just one of the more dramatic examples of this increasing diversity, in the California State University system from 1983 to 1989, the proportion of women increased from 34 to 54 percent, of African Americans increased by 7.4 percent, of Asian Americans increased by

57.5 percent, and of Mexican American and other Hispanic groups by 49.4 percent (California State University, 1992; as quoted in Goldstein, 1994).

This growing diversity reflects changes in society at large. In some cases, the changes are actual growth in one segment of the population, Hispanics and Asians being prime examples. In other cases, the increasing numbers in institutional enrollment parallel increases in participation by groups in other institutions. The growth in female college and university enrollment, for example, mirrors the greater participation of women in the work force. Inclusion of persons who are physically challenged likewise reflects advances in their inclusion in society at large.

Advocates of multiculturalism argue that what is taught, who teaches, what is recognized as legitimate research, and who staffs higher education should more fully recognize these demographic shifts. Such approaches would bolster learning through increased self-esteem and related psychological benefits to students, would increase the interest and commitment of subordinate group students to completing higher education, and would fulfill a right of each student to be educated with reference to her or his own group experience.

The argument is based on the assumption that persons with similar experiences—particularly the experience of being a member of a subordinate group—can better teach or administer programs for students from that group and that they can serve as role models and provide motivation for students who are in the minority in higher education. In arguing that staffing, for example, should more fully reflect higher education enrollment, Plante and Atwell (1992) point out that diversity and inclusiveness have short histories in higher education. Even in an era when many campuses are attempting to do something about diversity, numerous faculty and administrators in the higher education power structure have little life-long experience with diversity. Indeed, most came through their own education when higher education was not diverse. In the 1950s and early 1960s, when many of today's senior faculty and administrators were in graduate school, 94 percent of college students were white and 63 percent were men, while some of America's most distinguished universities would not admit Blacks and women. Thus, even the best-intentioned institution is limited unless it diversifies its staff to more closely match the experience of contemporary students.

A second theme of the multicultural proponents is that all students should be prepared for a diverse future. Advocates of multiculturalism assume that society will continue to grow more diverse with continuing demographic trends toward higher numbers of nonwhites. Goldstein (1994) points out that California, the center for increasing diversity, will have a population that by the year 2000 is one-third Hispanic and one-seventh Asian, with a workforce that is 60 percent persons of color, while its retiree population is 75 percent white. A related assumption—again based on current trends—is that the workforce and workplace, whether office, factory, or school, will be more diverse and it is therefore of benefit to prepare today's students for careers in this diverse workforce. A further assumption is that the direct experience of diversity plus an expanded curriculum that tells all students about subordinate groups and their experience will help to ensure that graduates are better prepared to work in a diverse society.

The experience of some higher education institutions during the last few years demonstrates how unprepared many students are for a future of diversity. In the fall of 1992, following racial incidents and a history of racial tension at the University of Massachusetts at Amherst, a U.S. Department of Justice mediation team came to the campus. The racial strife was attributed to the lack of cultural sensitivity and the racial bias of many white students, 60 percent of whom come from the eastern part of the state, which has a history of racial intolerance. Administrators describe students as never having learned the basic issues of respect across cultures (DePalma, 1992).

A third theme says that multiculturalism should give voice to the previously voiceless. Many proponents of multiculturalism argue that adding the published works of those traditionally unheard from will give insight into current issues and can instill pride in subordinate groups. They argue that the traditional canon does not open the door to studies of those who are thought to be voiceless. Therefore, in the humanities, for example, students should read of people previously without authority or recognition, of people who have been disenfranchised or without power.

The pragmatic side of this argument is that the previously voiceless are being heard in society and their voices and interests must now be listened to and articulated in higher education. For example, as states elect more African American or Hispanic state legislators, one can expect that proposals for multicultural requirements for students at state universities will be more likely to succeed.

A fourth theme is that multiculturalism is really about structural change. Auletta and Jones (1990) describe a conflict in higher education in which multicultural proponents are pitted against European American proponents. The multiculturalists argue that higher education should prepare students for participation in an increasingly diverse society. The European American proponents argue that radical change in higher education is not necessary to prepare students for the future; existing theory and legacies can be expanded to include a multicultural perspective.

However, the conflict between the European American proponents and the multicultural proponents goes much deeper than an argument about what is sufficient to prepare students for diversity. The conflict has far more to do with power and structural relationships, Auletta and Jones argue. They base their analysis on the concept that a society's powerful forces—we would say dominant groups—use education to reproduce their own culture for their own benefit. The culture thus reproduced helps to maintain the ruling group in power. Thus, the debate is not one of diversity or no diversity, but one about whose vision of society will be promoted by higher education. The stakes in the debate are so important because retention or change in political power is riding on the outcome. This analysis affirms that some conservative critics are correct when they claim that multiculturalists have a political agenda beyond diversity.

Auletta and Jones conclude that the influx of "new students" in the 1960s coming into higher education did not just represent a more diverse group of people to be educated. Rather they articulated a challenge to a system that had supported Western European dominance for centuries, asking questions like "Who is entitled to be educated?" "What should be taught?" "How should it be taught?" "Who should do the teaching?" These students wanted change: curriculum revision, more faculty of color, more female faculty, knowledge relevant to their communities that they could take back to those communities, and courses taught in the community. These changes would make elite knowledge available to the masses. To some extent, ethnic studies were a result of this influx. Today, however, the movement for change also comes from faculty and others who promote multicultural approaches to the curriculum.

Institutions Which Have Adopted Multicultural Requirements

Colleges and universities have responded to the multiculturalists' call in a number of ways. One response has been to institute a diversity requirement of some type for first-year students or for graduation. In some cases many students take one required course that focuses on racism, gender, ethnicity, and other group differences and similarities. In yet other institutions, multicultural themes or lessons are integrated into requirements such as a first-year composition or literature course. In other cases, the requirement has been broader, with one or more courses required from a group that includes group (ethnic, women's) studies, international studies, cross-cultural studies, or anthropological studies.

What is at issue—and what we will see by looking at several case studies— is that the broadening of multiculturalism to include many students and the open and public discussion that this involves is a political process. The success or failure of the change effort often depends on how the effort is framed and presented or on factors outside the control of those promoting the change. Here we look at three cases, ranging from one that started successfully to one that aborted.

In some institutions the multicultural requirement has been quite specific and has been accompanied by rigorous preparation of special courses to meet the requirement. This was the case at the University of California at Berkeley. In 1989 the Berkeley faculty voted to establish an "American Cultures" requirement that mandated that every entering first-year student take one course that examines how America's diverse culture makeup has shaped the country's history, society, and identity (Magner, 1992). Approved courses had to deal comparatively with at least three of five groups: African Americans, American Indians, Asian Americans, Chicano and Hispanic Americans, and European Americans. Thus, the requirement was not an ethnic studies requirement or a requirement for a mandatory course on racism or foreign cultures. It was instituted to deal with the development of North American identity.

The university's goal was to have 120 new or revised courses developed by 1995. Course development was to be done through summer seminars on course development sponsored by the Center for the Teaching and Study of American Cultures. The four-week seminars brought in faculty who were given a stipend and who had to submit a proposal for a course. Courses were to be approved by a committee. Faculty and student acceptance appears to be fairly high after the first few years. Several factors have contributed to this success. First, the student body is diverse, with about one-third of the student body Asian, one-third white, one-fifth Hispanic, and one-twelfth African American. Second, the requirement did not focus on one group or on grievances, but on creating courses that show how diverse groups interact within American society. Finally, the university provided considerable planning and resources to enable faculty to design successful courses to meet the requirement.

At the University of Oregon, although a new requirement was instituted, the debate over a multiculturalism course brought bitterness and divisiveness to campus. As we will outline below, the debate demonstrates how many other issues enter the debate and how skillful politics are required to overcome the objections of those scared off by multiculturalism (Leatherman, 1994b).

The Oregon faculty first passed a multicultural requirement in 1988. The "Race, Gender, Non-European Requirement" mandated that students complete one three-credit course out of an array including courses such as introduction to cultural anthropology. When the university decided to revisit the requirement, a committee appointed by the university's president proposed two required courses, one focusing on contemporary race relations and one on race, class, and gender. The committee, the plan, and the cost all came under attack. One faculty member observed that the debate took on a life of its own, symbolizing everything that people felt was wrong on the campus—from money problems to weak faculty governance. Some felt the debate was about who was to control the curriculum, even about who was to control the university.

The faculty senate first approved the plan, then voted to reconsider it. After name-calling and other incidents ensued, the faculty senate decided a new group should attempt to put together a proposal. The new group was racially diverse, but included professors who had been at Oregon for a long time, who were in the hard sciences, and were politically mainstream. It had only one student member. The plan they developed had no stated price tag. It required students to take courses in two of three areas: American cultures, pluralism and tolerance, and international cultures. European Americans were added to the four groups students could study. Critics said the new proposal did not ensure that students would take courses dealing with race relations.

At Oregon, the multicultural effort became entangled with larger issues of control of the curriculum and finances. Nevertheless, a requirement was finally passed when created by a mainstream committee which most in the campus community perceived to have no political agenda of its own. The requirement as passed was also very broad.

A third case—at the University of Texas at Austin—demonstrates how a change effort can quickly lose support and abort. In 1989, responding to unhappiness about English 306, the one required composition course at the university, Texas hired a new director. She proposed that starting in the fall of 1990, English 306 focus on issues of differences and use judicial opinions as examples of arguments about race and racial preference. After a good deal of discussion, some voiced opposition, and with general enthusiasm and support from the dean of the College of Liberal Arts, the appropriate committee authorized moving forward with the course.

Opposition formed immediately. Some English Department faculty launched a media and letter-writing campaign that called the course ideological, racial, biased, and propagandistic. The course became the focus for opposition to multiculturalism on campus, within Texas, and in the national media. Moderate opposition questioned building writing courses around politically charged topics. The perception that the course had been developed to deal with campus racism turned against proponents as the course was portrayed as primarily attempting to indoctrinate. There was resentment by one department about the publicity— even if negative—the course received. Changing the most controversial text planned for the course did not quiet criticism. A "bring something Texan to burn" party by some English faculty enraged many people.

Despite strong votes of support by the English Department and graduate students who would teach the course, the university administration refused to authorize a field test of the course. Lack of general faculty support for the course meant little opposition to the administration's decision. Much of this lack of support by the faculty came from the faculty's identification of the course as a multicultural effort and their related belief that multiculturalism is a code word for intolerance. The controversial text and its definition of racism, the elitism of the "burn something Texan" party, and the very large scale of the change also contributed to the lack of support by faculty who might not have had objections to an individual faculty member teaching a multicultural course using any materials he or she chose (Getman, 1992).

Multiculturalism: A Threat to Ethnic Studies?

Increased attention to multiculturalism has raised issues of curriculum change and diversity. In many colleges and universities, including those in the above case studies, the core curriculum has added new voices and there are some efforts to require students to have a course or courses that include study of racial, ethnic, gender, and other groups. At the same time, traditional disciplines and their departments, especially in the humanities and social sciences, have sought to add faculty and courses that reflect multicultural concerns. These efforts to promote multiculturalism would seem to parallel and strengthen the rise and growth of ethnic studies programs. In fact, in the 1990s some scholars have begun to ask whether multiculturalism is a threat to ethnic studies.

Some ethnic studies scholars see themselves under attack. They view the push for diversity of the curriculum as substituting a good understanding of one group for superficial understanding of many and believe that well-intentioned academics have joined conservative critics against ethnic studies. They worry that multiculturalism and integration of ethnic studies into the curriculum may represent a move toward the kind of depoliticized ethnic studies that developed for European groups. They also worry that with expanded attention to multiculturalism throughout higher education institutions, ethnic studies may be co-opted or swallowed. If ethnic studies are integrated into the curriculum, there is concern that critics may promote the argument that separate ethnic studies are no longer needed.

The interest in diversity may be manifested in a push to get ethnic studies perspectives and scholarship into the mainstream curriculum through hiring ethnic studies scholars in departments such as history, political science, and literature (Hu-DeHart, 1993.) This was the case at San Francisco State University, where African American students protested the course taught by a new black faculty member in the political science department. The students viewed the course as essentially duplicating a course that had been taught in Black studies for years. The chair of Black studies felt the course in political science was a way for the administration to farm out what should be Black studies courses to "European" departments. He claimed it was doing so under the guise of multiculturalism and affirmative action (Magner, 1991). As the situation escalated, the ethnic studies professor cited the academic senate's policy against course duplication and the need to manage budget resources carefully. The new political science department cited academic freedom as the rationale to offer the courses they wished to offer. While the specific situation was resolved through the retitling of one of the courses and mutual discussion of the content, the San Francisco State controversy raises a number of issues:

- As more traditional departments integrate multicultural perspectives and develop multicultural courses, how should colleges handle the duplication or similarity among courses? How can the issue be defined as one of academic freedom and departmental autonomy?
- Is the movement to "mainstream" multicultural perspectives seen as an alternative, or as an addition, to the ethnic studies department? In short, is it a thinly veiled attempt to abolish ethnic studies? What is the role, position, and status of the ethnic studies department in the university?
- Will scholars gravitate toward more established disciplines rather than ethnic studies?

In addition to bringing more diverse faculty and courses into traditional departments, another initiative toward a more multicultural campus is to require students to take a specific course on diversity. The case studies from Berkeley and Oregon represent such requirements. Some ethnic studies scholars have opposed the idea of broad ethnic studies requirements, claiming that to implement such a requirement would put a strain on ethnic studies or dilute their offerings. As the chair of the program at Berkeley said, "We don't want to be a service station" (Magner, 1991).

- Should ethnic studies courses be required as part of a core curriculum or general undergraduate requirement?
- Do curriculum integration projects for faculty offer a more viable means for promoting integration of ethnic studies into the curriculum without straining ethnic study resources?

Bowser, Auletta, and Jones (1993) picture ethnic studies as "on trial," held in contempt, and marginalized. Multiculturalism may very well be a way to cut ethnic studies programs. They advise college and university departments that are growing more diverse to

- consult with ethnic studies if a new faculty person who will teach similar courses is being hired

- raise issues of ethnic studies as teaching is carried out from a multicultural perspective
- explore the option of having new faculty members teach in ethnic studies programs
- see the relation between multicultural education and ethnic studies as writing across the curriculum has been related to the English department

Similar conflict has arisen in fields beyond individual institutions. Multiculturalism has been particularly contentious, for example, in American Studies. The field has found itself split between those with interests in race, class, and gender—often minority scholars—and those with more traditional American Studies interests: religion, business, and the Constitution. The multicultural critique of American Studies sees it as treating race and ethnicity from the perspective of whites toward minorities and of viewing minorities as victims. Others within American Studies believe that the field is putting too much emphasis on race, ethnicity, and gender at the expense of scholarship and of giving full airing to conservative perspectives (Winkler, 1992).

Conclusion

In this chapter we have given a broad overview of multiculturalism, including the critiques offered by many within and outside of higher education. We then traced the development of an earlier effort in the 1940s and 1950s to bring a much less political approach to diversity to college and university campuses. We saw that proponents of multiculturalism are concerned with a number of themes, ranging from students' preparation for diversity to the curriculum's reflecting the nation's diversity to multiculturalism as structural change. Three case studies demonstrated alternative models of integrating multiculturalism widely in the university (specially prepared courses that examine diversity and society, the choice of one course from a wide range of courses on different cultures, and a first-year writing course centered around diversity). The case studies also showed how the implementation or failure to implement such changes is a complex political issue. We also raised questions as to whether multiculturalism and related efforts to bring diversity into departments, fields, and the curriculum might threaten ethnic studies by eliminating the need for such programs or by diluting ethnic studies as they attempt to serve a focused and increasingly large number of students. In chapter 4 we turn to a closer examination of ethnic studies.

The Emergence and Status of Contemporary Ethnic Studies Programs in the United States

This chapter provides an introduction to the growth and development of a select group of contemporary ethnic studies programs in the United States. These programs developed in concert with events and social pressures to diversify and increase female, lower socioeconomic, and ethnic and racial minority participation in higher education over at least a thirty-year period following the Second World War. For example, financial assistance for college and university study, in the form of GI benefits for serving in World War II and the Korean War, enabled more ethnically and socioeconomically diverse students to attend. In the 1950s, Supreme Court decisions like *Brown v. Board of Education* challenged separate-but-equal schooling for Blacks and focused attention on minority access to all educational institutions. These and other events and influences led to enrollment diversity, at first among white males from the middle class and from various geographic regions, followed by white females and minority males. The result was an expansion in the composition of those enrolled in higher education. Other events followed. In the 1960s, disenchantment with colonialism and the war in Vietnam and support for Third World liberation and civil rights raised questions about the treatment of the disenfranchised and underrepresented. Thus it was the new access opportunities afforded to some, along with a combination of international and domestic events, over several generations, which encouraged a diverse student body to pursue educational opportunities heretofore limited. Once inside higher education institutions, these students raised questions about the relevance of higher education to world events and to their communities and about the still-limited minority representation in higher education.

To begin the discussion, it is important to note that until the Second World War, higher education in the United States was an aspiration of relatively few individuals, with access clearly biased in favor of a segment of white males. Colleges and universities were associated with a small portion of the population, primarily because the economy was labor intensive and not many individuals were required to be schooled beyond a high school diploma. World War II, however, brought changes that had a profound impact on the need for post-secondary education. The knowledge base for industry and manufacturing within an emerging global marketplace increased the need for formal education in many careers. Thus, during this period higher education took on more importance as the "gatekeeper" for many careers, often making it necessary to secure college training to prepare for occupations. Hundreds of thousands of military personnel, out of the service and provided with government assistance, enrolled in the nation's colleges and universities. The war experience increased the expectations of these veterans, including many African Americans and Hispanic Americans, who were made aware of educational opportunities that were formerly either unknown or unavailable. The war also brought many women into the workforce for the first time, and while many were forced out of jobs by returning veterans, their position in society and their expectations about careers were also raised.

Higher education enrollments grew rapidly immediately after the war. There were several federal initiatives designed to assist veterans to return to what had become a rapidly changing society, including the Servicemen's Readjustment Act of 1944 and the GI Bill of Rights. While enrollments ultimately leveled off in the late 1940s, they exploded again in the late 1950s and into the 1960s, partially as a result of demography and partially due to support from the Defense Education Act of 1958, the Civil Rights Act of 1964, and the Higher Education Act of 1965. Again, many of the individuals who took advantage of the opportunities to attend college were from formerly underrepresented segments of the population. The enrollment growth also reflected the new challenges in the world as the Cold War and U.S. technical competition with the Soviet Union fueled growth in higher education. This occurred not only in the sciences but in the professions, foreign languages, and fields related to technical assistance to the developing world. And because of the worldwide impact of the relationships between education and the economy, such enrollment growth was not restricted to the United States. Between 1950 and 1964, for example, the number of students enrolled in higher education doubled in the United States, tripled in France, doubled in West Germany, and went up 60 percent in Britain and 50 percent in Italy (Stolze, 1988). Total enrollment in higher education in the United States increased from 2.5 million in 1948–1949 to 3.4 million in 1958–1959 and to over 7.6 million in 1968–1969. While the news of Sputnik and the resulting National Defense Education Act spurred college enrollment growth in the 1960s, so did the accessibility of higher education (Ferrin, 1971).

For minority populations and their access to higher education, the 1964 Civil Rights Act was especially significant. From this initiative came the now familiar TRIO programs—Upward Bound, Special Services, Talent Search—as well as Executive Order 11246, which created the policies associated with affirmative action (Wilson, 1994). As with the GI Bills, most of these initiatives were intended to increase access and success in postsecondary institutions. These policies, however, primarily assisted whites, African Americans, and Hispanics rather than Asian and Native Americans. Asians were not numerous enough to attract special consideration until they increased their immigration rates to the United States following a 1965 revision to the immigration laws. This immigration was not seen in higher education enrollments until the 1980s. In contradistinction to the others, Native American enrollment remained relatively flat and thus, for the most part, went unaffected by these efforts (Kidwell, 1994).

By the middle of the 1970s, many saw that access to higher education alone for minority populations was not sufficient. Rather, it became apparent that special efforts were needed to increase the likelihood that such students would receive the special assistance they needed to improve their graduation rates and lower the probability of dropping out. Postsecondary institutions began to define the problem as one of retention and placed more attention on tutorial services, learning assistance and basic skills centers, and child care (de los Santos Jr. and Rigual, 1994). In the late 1970s and early 1980s, however, many of the same issues remained. Astin (1985), for example, through a Ford Foundation study conducted in 1981, found that institutions were often indifferent to minority student needs. They were reported to have lacked effective instructional programs designed to promote cultural awareness and identity and to develop bilingual skills, and they had inadequate academic and career counseling services. The national advisory committee that worked with Astin recommended that there be an enrichment of services for minority students, that centers for social and educational exchange be designed to promote identity and pride, that academic support services be enhanced, and that ethnic studies programs be increased.

By the 1980s the momentum that had characterized enrollment in higher education for the previous twenty-five years began to slow. The proportion of African American high school graduates between 18 and 24 years who enrolled in postsecondary education decreased from 39.8 percent in 1976 to 30.3 percent in 1988, and for Hispanics the rate fell from 50.4 percent to 35.3 percent over the same time period (American Council on Education, 1989). Although these differential enrollment-rate reductions by population groups were apparent, when placed in historical context they could not mask the above-mentioned overall growth in higher education enrollment over a forty year period.

The growth of local two-year colleges, for example, was dramatic as state and local leadership realized that private four-year higher education institutions could not meet the demand. From 1958 to 1968 a new public two-year college opened on the average of every two weeks in the United States (Ferrin, 1971).

The two-year colleges were to meet barriers to access by being free or charging very low fees, by offering "open admissions," and by locating in densely populated urban areas. While they initially served a wide and diverse population, community colleges in recent years, because of their urban locations and lower cost, have evolved in many areas to be much more heavily enrolled by minority populations than four-year institutions.

The rapid expansion of higher education meant that equality of access was achieved for some white ethnic groups who had previously been among subordinate groups in higher education. In 1916, for example, there were only 32,000 students enrolled in Catholic colleges, many of them in precollege programs. This number grew to 162,000 in 1940. The war brought what Greeley terms a "half dream and half nightmare," with too many students and too few faculty. Enrollment in Catholic higher education institutions reached 260,000 in 1960. By 1969, Catholic enrollment reached 400,000 and Catholics were then as likely as other North Americans to have gone to college (Greeley, 1969). This success exemplifies the character of most white ethnic immigrant groups as they moved out of subordinate status during this century.

However, the rapid growth in higher education also demonstrated how little success many minority groups had in gaining access to the nation's colleges and universities. Even in the late 1960s, African American access was still very limited and the number of African American faculty and administrators extremely small. For example, in a 1969 study of eighty of the most prominent state universities in the United States, African Americans represented only 2 percent of those enrolled, as compared to representing 12 percent of the total population (Ferrin, 1971). By the late 1970s, African Americans constituted some 4 percent of the faculty and 7 percent of the administrators. Much of this gain was due to employment on federal grants, and thus individuals in these positions typically had no security of employment. Furthermore, these employment figures also included professionals in the historically Black colleges and universities (Wilson, 1994).

It is with this history of enrollment increase and diversification that the ethnic-specific initiatives of the late 1960s and 1970s emerged. Such programs exist partially as a result of the dissatisfaction registered among minority students and faculty with their lack of impact on higher education, especially their lack of progress in participation and success in higher education, and partially by the wider civil rights and international liberation movements in the Third World. By the mid-1960s the Civil Rights movement was in full swing in the United States, and Third World peoples were rising up against colonialism, especially in Africa. The Vietnam War was also drawing worldwide criticism. Such events prompted students at San Francisco State in the fall of 1968 to form a coalition of separate ethnic action groups. This coalition was known as the

Third World Liberation Front. Among other demands, they rallied for the initiation of a Third World College at the University of California, Berkeley (Okihiro, 1991). Charges of racism, sexism, and elitism were clearly part of the student outcry against the status quo. These criticisms, in turn, led to the occupation of administrative offices, and in certain cases campus violence, to demand change in higher education through greater representation of the minority experience in the curriculum. Thus, while attacks on narrow student admissions and faculty recruitment and promotion criteria were visible manifestations of the minority agenda, behind the agenda lay the elimination of class privilege and bringing into the mainstream important aspects of the international and North American minority experience (Majek, 1991; Butler and Schmitz, 1992).

Ethnic Studies Programs

The roots of ethnic studies are found in the protests associated with the relatively poor socioeconomic and political status of minority populations in the United States. But even this basically antagonistic and conflictual orientation underlying ethnic studies is associated with some basic assumptions and beliefs regarding society and its future. First, the existence of ethnic studies in higher education is an implicit recognition that all societies are segmented vertically and horizontally, with the divisions associated with such characteristics as race, ethnicity, socioeconomic status, gender, and so on. Further, these segments are assumed to constitute important foundations for individual and group identity and for the general functioning of society. Second, there is general acceptance that the enrollment, curriculum, and personnel associated with a society's educational institutions, especially those supported by state or local governments, should reflect the diversity of the broader segmented society. The result has often been an emergence of individual ethnic studies programs as a manifestation of grassroots movements which challenged the academic status quo. Third, there is an assumption associated with the argument that interdisciplinary study and inquiry is important and necessary to connect scholarship and pedagogy with the real-world environment. Most programs attend to concepts like power, identity, access, and the like, but the extent to which curricula actually reflect interdisciplinary and cross-ethnic issues and relate to the community is variable. Some, for example, focus on a single discipline or ethnic group and remain isolated from outside struggles. Such practices vary from campus to campus and from discipline to discipline.

Fourth, there is an assumption of egalitarianism across ethnic and related segments, advocating the sharing of power and influence collaterally rather than placing power in the hands of one segment to be used selfishly or against others.

Thus, the practices of ethnocentrism, racism, sexism, classism, and segregation are to be addressed through ethnic studies with the goal of creating new and more positive relationships among and between peoples of all backgrounds. And, finally, there is an assumption that the formal higher education curriculum can be used as a vehicle to recognize the contribution of subordinate populations to the general welfare of society. Traditions of teaching and learning, records of particular experiences, and the application of differing perspectives on issues of general concern are all intended to enrich inquiry. Such a position assumes that ethnic studies curricula serve to raise consciousness and enlighten as well as lead to societal change (Butler and Walter, 1991). Hu-DeHart (1993) puts it this way: "Ethnic studies seeks to recover and reconstruct the histories of those Americans whom history has neglected; to identify and credit their contributions to the making of U.S. society and culture; to chronicle protest and resistance; and to establish alternative values and visions, institutions and cultures" (p. 52).

An interesting, but atypical example of an ethnic studies program that transcended national boundaries and which evolved over hundreds of years is Jewish studies. Its rapid growth in this century shows how ethnic studies can contribute to the construction of both a national and international identity. Jewish scholarship can be traced from the first century, with much of it before the seventeenth century focusing on the Hebrew language. The first major history of postbiblical Jewish life was published in the early 1700s (Adelman, 1991). Close to this time, Jews and Jewish studies entered the colleges and universities of the United States, where, for example, Hebrew was required at Harvard from its beginning. During the last quarter of the nineteenth century, interest in Hebrew paralleled the rapid expansion of the North American Jewish community and the spread of higher education in the United States. By the turn of the century, Jewish seminaries were established and Jewish studies was further grounded in United States' higher education. The founding of the State of Israel in 1948 furthered interest in Jewish studies such that by 1966 Jewish studies was offered at ninety-two United States' colleges and universities and by 1969 some six hundred students were reportedly majoring in Jewish studies. An important factor in the expansion and development of Jewish studies has been its existence for the preparation and sustenance of practitioners, both Christians and Jews (Adelman, 1991). This factor has also been associated with a major division in the field, dividing the ethnic from the disciplinary—the former preserving Jewish distinctiveness, and the latter addressing common questions extrinsic to particular Jewish needs and concerns (Neusner, 1987).

The case of Jewish studies points to the benefits that domestic ethnic groups gain from ties to their international homelands and with the promulgation of a common religious literature with the dominant group. Thus, even though ethnic studies programs are conceptually and substantively independent from international area studies, recent immigration patterns from Asia, Latin America, and Africa to the United States finds ethnic studies and international studies growing closer together. In addition, there are some populations—Mexicans, Dominicans, and Puerto Ricans, among them—who travel so frequently between their home countries and the United States that they make national boundaries all but disappear in their daily lives. Furthermore, as particular populations seek to understand their own history, some ethnic studies programs have taken a decidedly international turn. Afrocentric curricula, for example, expose early African history as a means to explore its impact on the experiences of African Americans living in the United States. Thus, while international studies has a broader agenda than connecting the historical roots of immigrant populations to their present status, including historical roles in technical assistance, public policy, arms control, and so on, one important overlap between ethnic studies and international studies is the connection between the history of the sending country and the encounter with the host or receiving country.

Ethnic studies grew in the late 1960s and 1970s partially because it was a period of overall growth in higher education and there were resources available to invest in program development, student aid, and the professional advancement of faculty, including being able to make special efforts to assist minority faculty members. Administrators who desired a calm campus as well as those who believed in the overall goals of ethnic studies programs found ways to create new ethnic initiatives. Sometimes these initiatives were taken under pressure and at other times voluntarily. Pressure, for example, was present at San Francisco State and the University of California, Berkeley, in 1968 as these institutions were among the first to respond to demands for greater access of minority students, the hiring of more minority faculty, and curricular changes.

Chandler (1993) reports on another case where pressure was applied by students and faculty to gain greater ethnic presence. The case involves California State University, Northridge, where in November 1968 a group of African American students seized the college president's office and held him and three dozen employees for three hours. Frustrated with a lack of response to their complaints, the students rounded up a group of administrators and marched them to the president's office. The president was then forced to sign an agreement committing the institution to establish an African American studies department on campus, recruit more minority students and employees, and not press charges against the students. After the dust settled, however, twenty-eight students were prosecuted for kidnapping and false imprisonment. Most were convicted, with some going to state prison and others to the Los Angeles County jail. The programs which appeared as a result of this kind of pressure, as well as those which were implemented voluntarily, ultimately began to communicate with one another and networks appeared. These networks helped member programs to leverage their influence and share information and resources. Professional associations like the National Association of Chicano Studies, the National Council for Black Studies, the National Association for Ethnic Studies, the American Indian Studies Association, and the Asian American Studies Association were among those begun at this time (Butler and Schmitz, 1992).

By the late 1970s, a wide variety of ethnic studies programs were being offered across the country. While most were located in California and most were associated with the Civil Rights movement and hence with larger minority populations, there were also a number of programs which focused on other groups. Because these others were predominantly white, European populations, it is also likely that such efforts emerged in reaction to minority ethnic studies or because their consciousness was raised about their own ethnic backgrounds and they took steps to reinforce those traditions. Washburn (1979), for example, in a survey of ethnic studies programs in the late 1970s, identified programs on Amish Americans in Ohio, Armenian Americans in Wisconsin, and Canadian, Czech, English, Filipino, German, Jewish, Polish, Slovak, Ukrainian, and Welsh Americans, among many others, spread across the country. In 1984, another survey of higher education institutions showed that 35 percent offered courses in African American studies, 24 percent in Asian and Pacific American studies, and 23 percent in Hispanic studies. This same survey pointed out that there were undergraduate majors in African American studies at 7 percent of all institutions, Hispanic studies at 6 percent, and Asian and Pacific American Studies at 4 percent. In 1992, there were approximately seven hundred African American, Asian and Pacific American, American Indian/Alaskan Native, and Hispanic studies programs. Most of these programs were founded at public, as opposed to private, institutions where accountability was more susceptible to public pressure from constituencies desiring ethnic studies programs (Butler and Schmitz, 1992).

The introduction and development of ethnic studies programs have been characterized by continuing debate, controversy, and sometimes conflict. Several issues appear to be at the center of concern. Most frequently cited has been the extent to which each field has an adequate knowledge base, as opposed to political pressure, to justify recognizing the program as a field of study. In the late 1960s and much of the 1970s this was a major issue for academic peers asked to approve courses of study. At that time, there had been relatively little systematic effort to organize and conceptualize the primary source material available on a particular ethnic group, and there was relatively little analytical or empirical scholarship on a group's current status. As a result of the often political rather than academic introduction of an ethnic studies program on a given campus, usually through student protests or community pressure, the issue of an available knowledge base took on even more scrutiny. The outcome was usually center or institute, rather than departmental, status for ethnic studies programs in the institution, typically used to test the extent to which the field would mature along the lines of more traditional academic programs. This meant that ethnic studies often emerged as a certificate program or as a minor field of study to complement or supplement a standard major in a discipline.

As programs continued to develop, status as an independent center or institute was viewed by some as an impediment to student and faculty recruitment, to the growth and development of ethnic studies as a bona fide field of study, and to the granting of regular university degrees. This has often led to additional conflict and controversy with departmental status becoming the goal of another round of political pressure from students, faculty, and the community. This remains as a major issue on some campuses in the 1990s. Some argued along the way that gaining acceptance in the academy would also mean a loss of integrity and autonomy and thus ultimately contradict the intent of some programs to be a lever for societal change. Even with departmental status, there emerged the question as to the ability of a program to stand alone with a focus on particular topics (e.g., the family) or theoretical and methodological approaches, as opposed to interdisciplinary status. Many universities have judged that ethnic studies, rooted in interdisciplinary competencies, needs to draw from the entire campus's resources rather than be localized in a single department. Again, controversy has emerged as to the extent to which a core faculty is needed to constitute a field of study as opposed to the coordination of a number of faculty members from various departments and their particular courses of instruction.

This issue of departmental versus interdepartmental status has also touched on the extent to which an ethnic studies program should become isolated from the rest of campus, with faculty and students who identify as members of the group being the sole or dominant participants. This has been an issue for some academic peers who are not inclined to support departmental standing for units where only those whose physical appearance or ethnic membership and identity are encouraged or even permitted to participate. Basically, as we indicated in the last chapter, the question is: Do you have to be a member of the ethnic or racial group to pursue inquiry or teach about that group? Magner (1993) reports that there have been several instances where individuals who do not identify as members of a particular group are held suspect by members of the campus community, usually the students. He reports, for example, that in 1993 at Iowa State it was not clear whether a white woman who was called racist and whose classes were protested was singled out because of her race or because of the lack of attention to Afrocentric theories. At Wayne State, he reports that a Tlingit Indian student filed a complaint against a non-Tlingit teacher for using terms like "squaw" in a Native American studies course. Similarly, he reports that students and community leaders at Portland State blocked a plan to name a white professor to head the Black Studies Department and at both Weber State and UC–Berkeley, students protested whites teaching Black history and race relations respectively.

Another issue that has confronted ethnic studies programs over the past two to three decades concerns the students attracted to ethnic specific courses. There is the argument, for example, that ethnic studies programs tend to attract individuals from the particular ethnic group under study and that rather than focusing exclusively on themselves they should be more broadly educated in the Western tradition. Thus, the argument goes, to educate individuals about their own history and culture in a narrow way is paternalistic, an irrelevant exercise in self-celebration and segregation that does not broaden the horizons of students. Another criticism of ethnic studies is that it contributes to divisiveness. The basis for this criticism comes from programs where there is emphasis on transparent political goals through ethnic and racial isolation purity and a unilinear approach to social and cultural study. This criticism finds fault with ethnic studies for its narrowness in not bringing forth common themes like family, poverty, and gender, all of which are sometimes thought to be best viewed from a comparative domestic, if not international, perspective. Yet another criticism argues that ethnic studies replaces one evil (Eurocentrism) with another evil (ethnocentrism). The argument is that students from all backgrounds need to develop a critical perspective and a deeper understanding of the complexities of modern-day living. Thus, some believe that the traditional canon as well as ethnic studies represent demagoguery and should not be followed.

African American Studies

Among the ethnic studies programs to have confronted such issues, the most prominent and the one typically viewed as the vanguard and the role model for others is African American studies. As an ethnic studies program it has probably struggled for legitimacy and credibility longer than any of the other contemporary minority-group ethnic studies efforts and continues to enjoy a dominant place among such programs. There is no clear consensus on the nomenclature to be used to refer to the field, and the literature suggests that it remains a topic of debate. "Black studies" was a dominant referent in the emergence of the field, but has since fallen in disfavor as not providing insight into the nature and character of programs. The common designations used at higher education institutions in the mid-1990s include "African American", "Afro-American", "African and Afro-American," and "Africana" studies. "African American" and "Afro-American" are often the terms used for programs focusing on the lifeways and history of African Americans living in the Western

Hemisphere or more typically in the United States. "African studies" is sometimes the preferred term for those institutions which desire to focus on the study of some or all of the people of the African continent. At times this implies a connection with the movement of those peoples to other areas of the world, while at others it signifies an international area studies focus on Africans exclusively. "Africana studies" appears to be the preferred term for those who wish to take a broad geographical reach, including all of the African Diaspora (Clark Hine, 1990). In the following discussion, we will generally use *African American studies* as the term of choice.

Harris (1990) identifies four stages in the development of what he terms *Africana studies* as an area of scholarly activity. These include the period from the 1890s to the Second World War, from 1939 to the mid-1960s, from the mid-1960s to the mid-1980s, and from then to the present. In the first stage, the late 1890s and early 1900s, in an attempt to document the history of African peoples, several small literary and scholarly organizations emerged to preserve and analyze their culture and status. It was during this period that Carter G. Woodson founded the Association for the Study of Afro-American Life and History (ASLAH), which went on to, among others, publish the *Journal of Negro History*, establish Negro History Week (now Black History Month), and the *Negro History Bulletin*. It was also during this period that W. E. B. DuBois pursued his ambitious plans to conduct research on the history of the Black experience in the United States. Through his professorial appointment at Atlanta University, he pioneered the systematic study of African Americans not only to document their life and history but to correct the biased nature of the writings to that date.

In the second stage (1939–1960s) of Africana studies proposed by Harris, he argues that there was a setback in the development of the field. To support his view, he points to the work of individuals like Gunnar Myrdal, whose scholarship in the 1940s failed to point to the unique nature of the cultural background of African Americans and expounded the belief that they, like white immigrants, would eventually be assimilated into the white-dominated society. This was a period when the social sciences themselves were testing theories of acculturation and assimilation, genetic versus environmental bases for social behavior, and the impact of colonialism and repression on the nature and status of domestic and international populations.

The third stage of development of Africana studies, according to Harris, is the period of explosive growth. From the mid-1960s to the mid-1980s, this was the era when the Civil Rights movement, Black identity, and the enrollment of Black students in higher education led to the formation of Africana studies programs. Fighting the "melting pot" thesis of subordinate-group assimilation to the dominant group, these newly enrolled students found ways to demand the inclusion of African and African American studies into North American higher education institutions and thereby challenge the Eurocentric nature of much of what was in college and university syllabi. They fought for degree and certificate programs and for departmental status, for special programs to recruit and support Black faculty and students, and for a larger voice in higher education's management structure.

During this period, the formation of Black studies programs ranged from an array of course offerings in various departments, the coordinated offering of courses through separate department contributions, some organized recognition of Black studies through full-time faculty coordination and the offering of courses. Combinations of the above, with joint appointments in Black studies and participating departments, research institutes, centers, and programs, along with traditional academic departments with a core faculty and degree-granting status were also present (Young, 1984). Throughout this period and to the present day, the goal has been to achieve departmental status on campuses, attempting thereby to be represented in a similar fashion to other academic units. At the end of this period, approximately the mid-1980s, Harris believes that legitimacy and institutionalization had occurred for Africana studies and that it was now time for more sophisticated analyses and interpretations of the African American past and present.

Cole (1991) argues that the growth and development of what she terms *Black studies* have always been associated with concepts like equality, civil rights, and ethnic identity, and thus to the politics of the time. Because Black studies traditionally involves the inclusion of a Black perspective and cultural identity within the dominant curricula, she ties its development to the fight by African Americans to demonstrate and challenge the status quo in North American higher education. The results of the critical appraisal given by protesters against the status quo, especially in the 1960s and 1970s, were corrections to the years of distortions and omissions on the life and status of African American peoples. But the impetus that gave rise to the development of programs during that period has also declined. In fact, Cole notes that the number such programs, after having reached a high of approximately 800 programs in the early 1970s, has dwindled to some 375 programs in the early 1990s. Further, she argues that strict financial constraints, difficulties securing faculty promotion and tenure, lack of academic counselors for students, and in some cases active counseling against Black studies as a field of study were all present to make further progress difficult.

A specific challenge to African American studies has been to make greater inroads into the historically Black colleges and universities (HBCU). In the eyes of some, such programs are not needed given the role models provided by the existence of black faculty on HBCU campuses. In the late 1980s and early

1990s, however, students on some HBCU campuses began to agitate for the establishment of African American studies programs. Tennessee State University in Nashville and North Carolina Agricultural and Technical University in Greensboro were two such institutions. In the former, a Department of Africana Studies was established and in the latter an African American Studies Program, with a course requirement in the undergraduate core curriculum, was implemented (National Council for Black Studies, 1994).

Among the issues confronting African American studies in the 1990s is continued departmentalization of its programs, agreement on a common knowledge base, the development of a core faculty, the recruitment and retention of students, and a general commitment to the betterment of the status and participation of the African populations, whether at home or abroad. These goals should not imply that some progress in such areas has not been achieved. For example, African American student enrollment increased from 1982 to 1992 by some 27 percent, with African American women increasing by 33 percent (Otuya, 1994). Nevertheless, it is a time of increased introspection. Harris (1990), for example, argues that it is time for African American studies faculty to return to asking basic questions about where they are and where they are going as a field of study—from intellectual commitments, to service and support of community initiatives, to increasing Black presence on campus, to ensuring that students be exposed to not only their own history but to that of other population segments.

Gates (1992) sees the status of African Americans in higher education in the early 1990s more pessimistically. He cites current efforts attempting to undo many of the accomplishments achieved during the past twenty-five years. Increased racial tension on campuses, downturns in enrollments, attrition, cuts in external financial support, and so on, are mentioned and associated with basic questions about how to ensure that the field has permanent institutionalization in the larger North American higher education establishment. Clark Hine (1990) sees a mixed landscape. On the positive side, she calls attention to the enormous strides made by scholars and researchers in the field and notes that there are more first-rate scholars working in the area than ever before. Yet, while she notes that this group of scholars will move what she calls "Black studies" to even higher levels of accomplishment, there are issues which need to be addressed. These include nomenclature; curriculum; identity, mission, and structure; graduate programs; faculty recruitment, retention, and development; accreditation; and professionalization. She also points to ongoing debates over whether Black studies is a field or a discipline. Further, there exists the difficulties in hiring full-time Black faculty, the challenge of a coherent curriculum including a consensus around what should be included in an introductory course, the level of degrees and certificates to be offered, and so on.

Some see the biggest challenge to African American studies in the 1990s being the nature and focus of study. As Clark Hine (1992) notes, that challenge is seen in the effort to reclaim and reconstruct the African basis of Western civilization. Thus, paralleling the debate over nomenclature mentioned earlier, the question for many in African American studies is the emerging Afrocentric focus of much of the scholarship and curricula as a continuing response to the Euro-American dominance of what constitutes valid knowledge. This challenge is creating controversy within the ranks of African American studies scholars, some of whom see in Afrocentrism a dogma of absolutism (Clark Hine, 1992). The basic characteristic of Afrocentricity is to move or bring into contemporary society and thus to the forefront all peoples of African descent. It focuses on exposing the Eurocentric manipulation of the African past. For example, Afrocentrism challenges the view that Egypt was a part of the Middle Eastern cultural basin and instead points to the contributions made by Black Africa to Egyptian civilization and to Greek philosophy. Thus, many of the accomplishments of the ancient world are said to have roots in Black Africa and attributable to African peoples. The more radical side of Afrocentrism seeks to empower African American students by having them adopt principles of their moral superiority over whites who are said to victimize them. It seeks to enjoin Blacks from throughout the world through a strong sense of identity to ensure that they have mutual support (Dei, 1994). Molefi Asante, one of the most quoted scholars associated with the Afrocentric perspective, has sought to place the individual as subject rather than object within the history of all peoples, with the intent of liberating the African peoples and their descendants from slavery, colonialism, and neocolonialism (Asante, 1991).

The Afrocentric perspective has given rise to a healthy debate on campuses and in the literature as to the vitality and viability of African American studies programs and scholarship. The more traditional approach to African American studies is criticized because of its closeness to the concepts and methodologies of traditional disciplines and thus to traditional Euro-American perspectives and frameworks. While earlier, the African American studies debate went on between such adversaries as Black Nationalists and Marxists, the current paradigms pose the more traditional, discipline-based approach against those who wish to dismantle and disassociate themselves from such frameworks. Afrocentrism is part of an effort to deconstruct the Eurocentric perspective and remove the constraints on inquiry into the history of Black people. Hall (1991) argues, however, that in itself Afrocentrism is insufficient to constitute a basis from which to build African American studies scholarship. He does so by pointing to the static and rather isolated way in which Afrocentrism presents its data, parallel to but not interacting with Western-dominated economic, cultural, and political structures. For example, he argues that Afrocentrism does not recognize any signs of acculturation and that the absorption of non-African customs and values have had only negative effects. He believes Afrocentrism has constructed a mythology that only parallels that of the mythology created on behalf of a Eurocentric approach. He calls for less of a focus on the past and more on the present and future, with an effort to synthesize rather than dismantle the characteristics of Black life. A related critic is Paul Gilroy (1994), whose work argues against the linear approach of many Afrocentrists. His own scholarship builds on the idea of a transnational culture and the centrality of the Black experience, especially slavery, to both the British culture and the North American culture. Thus, he seeks to bring forth the Caribbean and African experience to better understand how those influences shaped the nature of present-day Britain and the United States. He is especially critical of those who believe they can define cultures purely on the basis of race as he suggests Afrocentrists have a tendency to do.

Chicano Studies

Although underrepresented in higher education and in positions of power and influence in the occupational structure of the United States, Chicanos (individuals of Mexican descent living in the United States) constitute a major segment of the population, especially in the Southwest, where some 80 percent are resident. As with other minority populations, there is considerable heterogeneity among Chicanos, whose identity may be associated with differing backgrounds. Some, for example, have ancestors who were among the earliest Spanish to arrive in the hemisphere, others trace their lineage to families who lived in the area for more than a century, and others are associated with various waves of immigration coming north from Mexico during this century. It was these later waves of immigrants, moving further north in the United States, often to serve seasonal labor needs in agriculture, who constitute the now-sizable Chicano population in the West, Southwest, and Midwest. Attachment among many Chicanos to Mexico has also remained strong, with considerable movement back and forth across the border.

The first time that the presence of Chicanos as a group was highly visible nationally was during the ethnic revival period of the late 1960s. As it was for their African American counterparts, higher education was a focus of their efforts to gain greater identity, visibility, and access to the opportunity structure. Aguirre and Martinez (1993) argue that the Chicano movement of the 1960s represented an extension of the United States–Mexican War of the 1840s. That war resulted in the United States assuming control of the northern half of the country of Mexico and placing the existing Mexican population of that area under the political jurisdiction of the United States. They argue that the ethnic identity being sought in the late 1960s was a form of ultimate liberation from that colonial past.

Between 1960 and 1990, the Chicano population increased from 2.1 to 13.3 million and from 1.2 percent to 5.4 percent of the total U.S. population. In 1990, 5.4 percent of the Chicano population, compared to 39.9 percent of Asians, 28.5 percent of Whites, and 11.4 percent of African Americans, finished four or more years of college (Aguirre and Martinez, 1993). Among Hispanics living in the United States, more Cubans (20.2 percent) and Puerto Ricans (9.7 percent) achieved four or more years of college than did Chicanos. Chicanos are heavily concentrated in community colleges, where more than 60 percent of those attending postsecondary education are enrolled. Some of the issues associated with the relatively low school achievement of the Chicano population include a tendency to live in more segregated, low socioeconomic communities, place-ment in low achievement tracks in schools, and a high drop-out rate, averaging 50 percent over the last thirty years (Aguirre and Martinez, 1993). Given the common border with Mexico and the frequent contact with Mexican peoples and cultures, the Spanish language has been maintained by large sectors of the population and some say this has also acted as a constraint against learning English and school success.

Given this set of conditions, it is perhaps not surprising that Chicano students and faculty who have found their way into higher education have attempted to increase their presence and utilize their position to leverage greater access and power for members of their community. In 1968, Chicano high school and college students across the Southwest held marches and boycotts to show their solidarity for educational reform and greater access to the opportunities in the wider society. In the late 1960s, Chicano students and faculty organized at the University of California, Santa Barbara, to form the Coordinating Council on Higher Education (CCHE). This Council promulgated a plan, entitled "El Plan de Santa Barbara," designed to increase Chicano student representation in higher education, provide adequate funding for their support, and provide programs for faculty and student recruitment and retention. Subsequently, the organization known as MEChA (El Movimiento Estudiantil Chicano de Aztlan) was formed to pursue these same goals. In recent years, the Hispanic Association of Colleges and Universities (HACU) has taken up the educational needs of Chicanos, along with other Hispanic populations (Aguirre and Martinez, 1993).

As Chicanos increased their representation in higher education in the 1970s, the issues became more focused on how to increase relevant student services to raise the probability of academic achievement. Other issues included university-community relations and the establishment of academic programs which responded to student interests and characteristics. In the 1980s, the climate turned against minority education support nationally and there was a general downturn in efforts to respond to minority, including Chicano, needs. As pressures built in the 1980s to assist Chicanos into and through higher education, some states, specifically Arizona and Colorado, issued reports which, among others, identified the status of the education of Chicanos and called for new efforts to improve access, retention, support, curricular reform, and community relations.

As with African American studies, the basis for many Chicano programs and courses were created and offered by a variety of faculty across several disciplines. They were first implemented in California colleges and universities. The guidance and inspiration for this activity came from "El Plan de Santa Barbara," mentioned above, which contained model programs and courses and which presented the case for departmental status for such programs. The humanities, social sciences, and education were the focus for such programs and the emphasis was primarily on the undergraduate curriculum. Outcomes were to be increased identity for students and a greater appreciation for their cultural heritage. Efforts were aimed at encouraging Chicano students to work for and commit to interventions which would enhance the wider Chicano community. Ideologically, the Chicano studies movement was guided by a need for independence from the wider Anglo-American society and an enhancement of the socioeconomic conditions of the Chicano population.

In 1973 the National Association for Chicano Studies was founded as its member institutions desired to act collectively for Chicano interests. Underlying the professional network was a desire to enhance the identity of Chicanos, bring forth the Chicano culture, and demonstrate the years of struggle that the Chicanos had endured in attempting to succeed in a socially oppressive environment. Aguirre and Martinez (1993) argue that Chicano studies programs have had marginal success in higher education. They cite as an example the case of UCLA, where in 1993 Chicanos failed to persuade university officials to establish a department of Chicano studies. The situation at UCLA was reminiscent of the student-administration conflicts of the 1960s in that the conflict involved student marches, fasting, and violence as mechanisms to convince university administrators to make institutional changes.

UCLA has long had an organizational structure which placed ethnic and international studies as research and curricular resource centers rather than departments. The university's rationale for such a structure was that these programs were interdisciplinary in nature and that they needed facilitation by some university unit which would cross-cut disciplinary boundaries. In the 1993 case, the students at UCLA wished instead to establish a Department of Chicano Studies. The university administration commissioned a study which, among others, recommended against such an action. The reasons included UCLA's structure and the lack of academic substance in the program to justify an ethnic studies department. The students were upset with the conclusions and some three hundred protested. On one occasion, they confronted police. Subsequently, some five students participated in a hunger strike. The student-driven protest resulted in an agreement to establish interdisciplinary instructional centers, one of which would be named the Caesar Chavez Center for Interdisciplinary Instruction in Chicana and Chicano Studies. While this was viewed by some as a satisfactory resolution to the conflict, others perceived it as another case where departmental status was not achieved for yet another ethnic studies program (Henry, 1993).

Asian American Studies

The diversity of the Asian American community distinguishes it from both African American and Chicano communities in the United States. The community is composed of several national and regional populations—among others, Korean, Japanese, Chinese, Filipino, Vietnamese, and Asian Indian American groups—each of which is characterized by distinct linguistic and related cultural attributes as well as unique historical reasons for linking with the United States. With more than 60 percent of the Asian American community living in the United States being foreign born in the 1990s, many of these populations remain independent from one another and rely on their own membership for support and recognition. This diversity has challenged Asian American scholars, who are often second- and third-generation immigrants who are unable to communicate with members of this first-generation, heterogeneous, and recently arrived community.

Contemporary Asian American studies was initiated at the University of California, Berkeley, in 1969. At a time of the Third World strikes at San Francisco State and the University of California, Berkeley, Asian American students were involved in the issues of racism and colonialism and protests against the Vietnam War, and were taking steps to confront the injustices they saw in the United States and abroad. In the aftermath of the turbulence of 1969 and 1970, students and faculty organized the Asian American Political Alliance in 1971 and subsequently issued a manifesto outlining the rationale for a student movement which would work against forced acculturation and for increased identity and economic and cultural independence for Asian Americans in the United States (Okihiro, 1991). This was to be done through revising the curriculum and introducing courses focusing on the problems and issues confronting various Asian American populations. The first courses at San Francisco

State, for example, concerned Chinese and Japanese Americans (Mazumdar, 1991). As with other ethnic student movements of the period, there was considerable attention directed to the wider community as well, attempting to link higher education resources as a vehicle for bettering the lives of the wider population. The current organization representing the field is the Asian American Studies Association, with seven thousand members.

From the beginning of the movement in the 1960s, it was difficult to disentangle the international dimensions of Asian studies from the domestic focus on Asian Americans. Part of the explanation rests with the context of the late 1960s, when international events consumed the attention and concern of many students in the United States. Another part of the explanation rests with the difficulty encountered when attempting to study and understand, as with many other groups, the lifeways of Asian Americans without tracing their history to the countries and regions from which they came. Because of the recency of immigration of most Asian Americans and thus the importance of the connections between their national origins and current residence, for example, it is not surprising that separating Asian American studies from Asian studies is conceptually and historically difficult. Mazumdar (1991) cites three periods of Asian studies history, beginning in the late eighteenth century to the 1920s, the period from 1926 to 1968, and the post-1968 period. She notes that it was not until the last period, involving the rise of radical politics of the 1960s, that scholars began to take interest in issues such as racism and colonialism and began to confront the issues of connecting Asian with Asian American studies.

Mazumdar argues that even though many Asianists ignore or distance themselves from Asian American studies, there cannot be a separation of Asian studies from Asian American studies. Noted is the organization of Pacific Rim programs, which purposely explore the connections between East and West and recognize the economic and political interdependence which exists across the Pacific. She also argues that the identity crisis of Asian Americans, emerging primarily through assimilationist practices of the dominant population in the United States, and so prominent in the 1960s, has remained unresolved. Instead, Asianists have tended to leave alone topics such as race and racism and have typically found the politics of Asian American studies favoring protest and conflict to be alien to their scholarly pursuits.

Native American Studies

As with other ethnic studies efforts, Native American programs have struggled to achieve academic legitimacy within higher education while simultaneously attending to the student and community service agenda upon which many, at least originally, received their greatest support. While the study of American Indian issues may have a longer history than the study of most other ethnic groups in the United States, such a focus was traditionally the domain of anthropologists and linguists. Systematic programs in Native American studies, like their ethnic studies counterparts, received their major impetus for growth in the late 1960s. By the early 1980s, some 107 Native American studies programs were identified in two- and four-year institutions. Approximately one-half of these programs were either departments or administered through other academic units and offered either as academic majors or minors in Native American studies (Heath and Guyette, 1984).

The challenges evident in the growth and development of Native American studies are similar to those of the other ethnic studies programs: academic legitimacy; organizational presence; student and faculty recruitment and support; academic program planning and implementation; service to the community; and research and scholarship. Several of these have been especially difficult for Native American studies programs, however, because attempts to achieve these goals have come from a much smaller student and faculty population and from a longer period of dependency or colonized status in this country. Also distinct has been the relatively closer relationship Native American studies programs appear to have had with their respective communities and the expectations those communities have for their ethnic group connections in higher education.

Wright (1990) argues that this connection with the referent Native American community and the applied research and problem solving that has resulted has caused difficulty in developing a record of research and scholarship which is legitimate in academic institutions where such "action" or applied research is less common or acceptable. He believes that the need to develop research and scholarly activities remains as critical in the 1990s as it has since such programs made their push for institutional acceptability in the 1960s and 1970s. Both the quality of such inquiry and the contribution made to the knowledge base are identified as continuing challenges for Native American studies.

Given the low enrollment of Native American students in higher education, along with the relative paucity of faculty members, the recruitment and retention of both have become dominant issues in the development of Native American studies programs. Student support services have been especially important areas of commitment for such programs, given high drop-out rates and the sometimes difficult conflict the Native American student encounters between an identity with his or her cultural community and accommodating to the demands of higher education. Again, the explicit commitment made by Native American studies to the referent community can complicate the efforts of the program to achieve credibility within the higher education institution.

Concerning faculty, Wright points to the need to ensure that there are more qualified Native Americans who secure doctorates and, further, to ensure that once hired as faculty in higher education, their university or college reach out to ensure their professional development and thus their ultimate promotion and tenure. He recommends more graduate fellowships for students and more research support funds, released time for research, early leave policies, and mentoring by senior faculty for aspiring academics. Wright sees research and scholarship, followed by curriculum development, as the major challenges facing such new Native American faculty. He indicates that this means trading some of the service obligations to the institution, for which minority faculty are often called on to perform, for time to pursue these more central functions of inquiry and making Native American studies an important multicultural option in the general studies curriculum.

In a case study of the Native American Studies Program at the University of Arizona, one of the more well-developed and older programs, Strauss and Pepion (1992) identify some of the challenging issues facing ethnic studies and the higher education institutions where they are located. Although no program of Native American studies existed until 1968 at Arizona, there was a long history dating back to the founding of the university where Native American issues were represented in the institution's academic and service activities. The new effort was intended to strengthen Native American curricula and the number of Native American students and faculty. In the early 1970s, the Ford Foundation lent its financial and related support for the development of the program and saw its investment result in new degree programs and a general broadening of the university's commitment to Native American issues. As grant money from Ford dwindled and stopped, and the university was to assume responsibility for the programs, Strauss and Pepion argue that program status faltered and languished.

The Arizona program, according to the authors, still seeks academic legitimacy. They believe that the university failed to honor its commitments after the Ford Foundation funding stopped. They cite the fact that departmental status has not been achieved and promotion and tenure processes are not under the control of the program itself. The authors argue for the importance of external resources to ensure the long-term viability of such programs, especially in light of funding problems inside the institution. They also note that it is important for Native American studies to be recognized as a significant resource for interdisciplinary and multicultural studies and be placed organizationally where they can promote their interests and attract the support and attention of both the central administration and cooperating academic units.

Conclusion

An assessment of ethnic studies in the early 1990s presents a series of both common and distinct issues confronting their growth and development. It is clear, for example, that all seek greater legitimacy in higher education through a recognition of their scholarship, teaching, and service. In some respects, achievement of this goal is dependent on each institution's expectations for faculty and student achievement, the institution's tradition of interdisciplinary inquiry, and relations among and between racial and ethnic groups. For those programs that address this issue through the respected scholarship and teaching and hence the more traditional routes sanctioned by the academic community, the process will continue to be evolutionary and incremental. For others who seek to achieve legitimacy through more political, organizational, and, to some extent, symbolic means, like trading a center or institutional name and unit for departmental status, the goal may ultimately remain illusive. In effect, the program may achieve the symbolic goal, but the institution's faculty and students will know that the change was not granted as a result of sanctioned means.

As the search for acceptance of ethnic studies as an academic equal goes forth inside academe, the loss of the political agenda and community outreach so characteristic of the 1960s and 1970s will likely continue. Some argue that normal academic review processes for curricular change, promotion and tenure, and budget allocations have already pulled ethnic studies too far from its charge to enhance the socioeconomic and political status of members of the wider community. This diminution of the social action and social change agenda is fueled by academic scholarship often unintelligible to the community it was intended to serve. It is also paralleled by a fragmentation of the wider referent community as it accommodates and challenges the yet wider society to respond to its needs and interests.

The defensive posture on the part of what appears to be most ethnic studies programs, due primarily to the lack of acceptance by academic colleagues and the resultant aloofness from its wider ethnic community, is fed by the challenges faced by the individual programs. African American studies, while recognized as having achieved at the highest level among such ethnic studies programs, is now being challenged from within by Afrocentrism and its charge to radically revise and rewrite its knowledge base. Asian American studies is being torn by the recent heterogeneity of the immigrating populations in relation to those Asian American faculty in higher education who must represent and communicate with such diversity. The Chicano programs are also challenged by heterogeneity, as they must address the growing Latin American Hispanic presence that threatens to make Chicanos just one more Spanish-speaking population seeking identity in higher education institutions already characterized by little curricular space to address the wider society's pluralism. Even though Native American programs share this same challenge to address diversity, this is a longstanding issue for them, and one that is often dealt with by attending to local and regional tribes or units as opposed to national boundaries. African American, Chicano, and Native American programs are also perplexed by the need to increase enrollments by their respective populations. For Asian Americans, on the other hand, the issue is not increasing enrollment in higher education but avoiding the stereotype of setting the standard for achievement and the potential of reverse discrimination, especially on the West Coast, by confronting institutions which seek to cap or limit their enrollment in favor of providing access for other groups.

While each ethnic studies program is confronting distinct issues like those mentioned above, all are also attempting to build their respective historical traditions of scholarship and program development. All seek more of their own numbers, for example, to study and represent themselves to the outside world. For many African Americans this means rebuilding the African knowledge base, while for Asian Americans it means increasing their democratic inclusion in the United States as a racially distinct and varied population. Chicanos and Native Americans, at the same time, seek to increase their capacity, probably more than other groups, to solve the socioeconomic and political issues which confront their communities.

All of the ethnic studies programs are also concerned with their respective status relative to women's studies, multiculturalism, and international studies. Do they embrace, for example, the women's movement or the multicultural movement and use them as vehicles to present their history and culture to a wider student population through service courses? Or do they see women's studies as basically a comparative studies course with a focus on gender rather than ethnicity? Somewhat differently, do they see multiculturalism as a threat to further homogenize ethnicity and thus to lose ethnic identity and the tradition of building greater independence and autonomy? As to the international issue, where does one draw the line when the goal is to understand the nature of a group's domestic status when the roots of that group are so tied to another country? Fortunately or unfortunately, given academic governance, budgetary constraints, and social pressures from outside the institution, few will be able to make the decisions on these issues on their own. Such questions, however, are forcing ethnic studies programs and their respective higher education institutions to make difficult decisions about their reasons for existence and their goals.

Part 3

The Context and Strategies for
Addressing Diversity

Ethnic Studies, Multiculturalism, and the Social and Political Context: A Mirror to Society's Intergroup Relations

Ethnic and multicultural issues in higher education need to be addressed systematically and on multiple fronts, and involve the entire on- and off-campus community. Such a statement, while widely accepted, is seldom implemented. Other priorities, financial exigencies, and the day-to-day operations of an institution often interfere. Nevertheless, campuses and their wider communities often seek agreement on challenges that include

- the establishment of goals to diversify in demographics and programs
- the determination to investigate and resolve intergroup-relations issues promptly and fairly
- the continuous availability of cultural awareness training for students, faculty, staff, and administrators
- the infusion into the curriculum and extracurriculum of ethnic studies and multicultural studies and events
- the periodic collection of information to determine progress toward diversity goals

While there are many constraints on higher education to respond to such challenges, in this chapter we have chosen to concentrate on the social and political constraints on an intergroup-relations agenda. It is clear that higher education, whether private or public, cannot stray far or move too independently away from its various constituencies in implementing ethnic and multicultural studies. Given the divisions in such constituencies, however, institutions have difficulty knowing how to position themselves in the debate regarding multicultural and ethnic studies and how to come to terms with the decisions to move forward on program development. Such concerns face presidents, provosts, deans, and department chairs frequently as they weave their way through the potential minefield of educational decision making. We believe that it is oftentimes the external social and political context which most constrains the available flexibility for implementing policies and programs.

Social scientists have recognized the influence of society on schooling for some time. It is common for them to argue that a society's institutions reflect the dominant values and beliefs, organizational characteristics, and technology which are prevalent in their constituencies and the wider society. Often referred to as the "correspondence" principle, this dictum draws attention to the ways a society's institutions mirror the issues and concerns of the larger world from which they emerge and draw their sustenance. Because various segments of society (e.g., ethnic and racial groups, social classes) exert differing levels of political and economic influence, however, institutions are more likely to reflect the interests of the most dominant or powerful segments. It is often these more powerful outside interests, typically linked to government, business, and industry, which determine the agenda for institutions, especially the behavior of campus administrators. Thus, formal education is expected to mirror these and other interests in its organization, its decision-making structure, the emphasis placed on production and outcomes, and its commitment to both competition and cooperation. The same dominant-group economic and political influence (i.e., what is formally to be taught and learned); how teachers and students are to behave; the treatment of individuals by age, gender, race, ethnicity; and so on.

Challenging the dominant group, however, and also reflecting the correspondence principle, it can be expected that the less powerful groups in society will be heard. Thus, the development of ethnic studies and multiculturalism in higher education reflects the concerns of the community and region regarding intergroup and interpersonal relations. Pressures from Chicanos at UCLA and African Americans at Georgia State University for departmental status for ethnic studies and complaints from Asian Americans on the establishment of ethnic quotas on admissions in California are recent examples. We have seen this connection in earlier chapters as a result of enrolling a more diverse student body, the activities of ethnic and racial groups as they seek more status and identity, political and economic changes in other nations, and actions in the area of civil rights. In the 1960s, for example, these events—the Vietnam War, the ethnic revival movement, the Civil Rights movement—had rather profound effects on the emergence and change of ethnic studies and multicultural efforts in colleges and universities. One might surmise that events in the 1990s, such as the ethnic tension in Hawaii, Florida, and Massachusetts, war in the former Soviet Union, Haitian and Cuban refugees, and the conflict in southern Mexico between ethnic and socioeconomic groups, have an influence on intergroup relations in the United States and other countries.

In the 1980s and 1990s, for example, we have seen a dramatic shift in minority population movements from cities to the suburbs. This followed decades of so-called white flight from U.S. cities into surrounding neighborhoods at the perimeters. Between 1980 and 1990, for example, the black population in the suburbs grew by 34.4 percent, the Hispanic population by 69.3 percent, the Asian population by 125.9 percent, and the white population by only 9.2 percent. Those who changed residence were primarily middle- and working-class members of these minority groups who were moving up the socioeconomic ladder, escaping city life and seeking the suburban lifestyle. Affordable housing, better schools, and lower costs of living were often mentioned as pull factors, while escaping violence and the crowding of the inner city were mentioned as pushing people into the suburbs.

While suburbia in the United States remains dominated by whites—who comprise approximately 82 percent of the total suburban population—the greater visibility and opportunity for whites and minorities to interact is among the changing social and economic landscape which is reflected in schooling. It is this kind of change which shapes the nature and status of ethnic and multicultural programs. This chapter will provide a review of a sample of some of these external influences, most of which in the 1990s have established a highly contentious and growing conservative context within which ethnic studies and multicultural programs are challenged to grow and serve. The following chapter will then provide alternative approaches to change in higher education and for the implementation of intergroup-relations efforts.

Cultural Capital and the Competition for Access and Control

The late 1980s and early 1990s demonstrated an increasingly more visible rivalry and contentiousness among and between groups. Hunter (1990) argues that this characteristic of United States intergroup relations can be traced to the lack of a common set of assumptions about what constitutes right and wrong, good and bad, acceptable and unacceptable. Additionally, it seems that there is no overall consensus on what individuals and groups hold as the vision for themselves and others. The disagreements that are expressed, therefore, over abortion, child care, funding for the arts, affirmative action and quotas, gay rights, values in public education, or multiculturalism and ethnic studies emerge from different ideas about what criteria to use in making value judgments. These differences have created competition and conflict in higher education programs between placing emphasis on similarities as opposed to differences among cultural groups.

Merelman (1994) argues that there is a pervasive, enduring, and increasingly severe conflict across cultural boundaries in recent years, which he predicts will likely exist into the future. He believes that this conflict is due to the growing importance of what is termed *cultural capital* in shaping political and economic power and authority. Cultural capital consists of both technical skills, formal schooling, and knowledge of the symbols and talents which represent those who have power and influence and which are marketable in the employment structure. He goes on to argue that many members of minority ethnic and racial groups, because of their status and power, find themselves at a significant disadvantage relative to whites in gaining access to cultural capital, both through formal educational institutions and through what constitutes the day-to-day behaviors found most often among the middle and upper classes. Ethnic studies and, to a lesser extent, multiculturalism in education challenge the dominance of middle- and upper-class cultural capital in that they seek approval for integrating alternative perspectives and frames of reference for what constitutes the traditional knowledge base of formal education.

Brownstein (1994) assists us in understanding better how cultural capital is controlled by arguing that the dominant group naturally seeks to retain its ability to impose its standards of behavior on everyone. Such standards insist, for example, on both uniformity of treatment, or minimum standards on everyone irrespective of circumstance (e.g., new national educational standards which set uniform expectations for rich and poor students alike), and certainty of treatment, by restricting government institutions (from schools to courts) from granting exceptions to established standards (e.g., holding members of Congress to the same laws as other citizens). In the context of the challenges being thrust at the dominant group to share more broadly what constitutes and who controls cultural capital, the interest in establishing more and firmer standards may well be a backlash against countermovements like ethnic and multicultural studies. The common-standards agenda of the dominant group directly challenges the idea that racial and ethnic differences need to be brought forth, recognized, and used to ensure greater minority access and success while also celebrating them through areas like multicultural and ethnic studies. Thus, the battle lines are drawn between those who argue that attention should be given to how policies affect the whole while others argue that they should be directed to how they affect specific groups.

The concept of cultural capital is perhaps best seen as divided in parts and dependent on identity, access, and experience, rather than as being possessed entirely by one group. Two examples seem appropriate. One concerns the emerging distinctions within ethnic groups, involving primarily how an individual identifies as a group member and to which group he or she wishes to be identified. Each affects the acquisition of cultural capital. For example, *Asian* no longer refers to only Chinese, Japanese, Koreans, and Filipinos; it can also include Vietnamese, Cambodians, Hmong, and Laotians. Thus, from the perspective of identity, being "Asian" now is considerably more complicated both from the inside as a member and from the outside as an observer. Similar statements can be made regarding terms like *Latino, Hispanic,* and *Black* and the changing nature of each of their respective referent groups. Increased differentiation is also being made more apparent within single ethnic groups. For example, until the appearance of Clarence Thomas as a conservative nominee for the United States Supreme Court under the Bush administration in the early 1990s, African Americans were said to be perceived by many North Americans primarily as a single, relatively homogeneous, and politically liberal bloc. In effect, increased educational and economic variability, along with a differential impact in the marketplace seen in fields like the professions and the arts, and accompanied by the addition of new immigrants, has caused a transformation of both in-group identities and outside characterizations. African Americans and the immigration of blacks from Africa and the Caribbean and Chicanos, Puerto Ricans, and Cubans and the immigration of other nationalities from Central and South America are examples. The distribution of cultural capital across such socio-economic and ethnic and racial lines is obviously complicated and not easily disentangled at the group level.

An example of this complexity can be seen in an analysis of the achievements of women in the United States in the last twenty years. Bernstein and Cock (1994) document the progress achieved by women during this period, including their majority presence as undergraduate and graduate students, their increased presence as members of higher education faculty, and the literal explosion in scholarship and course offerings concerning women. But such achievements are masked, they say, by the use of the term *women*. For, underneath the term, and divided by age, race, ethnicity, and socioeconomic status, there remains considerable variation. African-American women, Latinas, and American Indian women trail far behind white women in all of these achievements. In fact, when the statistical figures are dissected, the authors report little progress achieved by women of color as undergraduate students, and mixed gains as graduate students. Thus, the authors conclude that policies like affirmative action have benefited primarily white and not other women. As the authors unmasked the scholarship and teaching activity in the area of women's studies, they also found that such efforts remain focused primarily on white women of privilege. Such conclusions point toward the unequal distribution of cultural capital among women both in achievement and as the focus of scholarship.

Related to cultural capital and a common standards agenda in daily life is what we referred to in chapter 3 as "political correctness". In the 1990s it became a heated area of serious debate as well as the target of humor and satire. According to Berman (1992), political correctness was originally a phrase associated with those who were staunch supporters of the Leninist left. It was then picked up and pursued by a seemingly contradictory set of followers. He says that, in the name of "sensitivity" to others, and under the potential of being labeled a sexist or racist, political correctness has resulted in adherence to a specific code of speech and behavior. This kind of intimidation has lead, says Berman, to the adoption of one language in private and a different, often euphemistic one, in public. According to critics, the "P.C." movement is not dissimilar to the McCarthy era of the 1950s, except that it emanates from the liberal left rather than the conservative right. Some argue that political correctness produces an atmosphere of repression in intergroup relations which is best seen on university campuses, and involves hyper-ethnicity, ultimately leading to the emphasis on uniqueness and identity in formal education and to the disintegration of the bonds that hold a campus together.

There are several ways to assess the meaning of political correctness according to Morley (1995). Among them is, first, the usage among those on the political left who hope to raise to a level of consciousness the implicit racism and sexism contained in our day-to-day vocabulary. A second and more explicit meaning of political correctness concerns attempts to control "hate speech" or the application of coercive measures like speech codes, typically on college and university campuses, to curtail offensive speech. A third usage of political correctness, according to Morley, is the use of the term by conservatives to refer negatively to almost any public expression that might be remotely termed liberal. This is a way at negating both the messenger and the message. Fourth, Morley says, the broadest usage of the term is in its mode as a means of social discretion or decorum. In effect, this usage is a way to indicate that it has become "good manners" or morally serious to be politically correct. The final application of political correctness takes on religious overtones, says Morley, as it gets connected with secular Puritanism—or a means to save souls through language. He goes on to credit the political correctness phenomenon with instilling a self-governing civility into everyday language as well reinforcing an appreciation for the First Amendment. Berman (1992) notes that political correctness was strengthened on the North American scene through a backlash against individuals like William Bennett and his successor, Lynne V. Cheney, who in the 1980s were the back-to-back chairs of the National Endowment for the Humanities. They ushered in a conservative agenda to apply criteria for determining acceptable scholarship and school curricula in the social sciences, history, and literature.

Scott (1991) argues that at the core of political correctness are the questions of what counts as knowledge and who gets to define what counts as knowledge. Such issues are central to ethnic and multicultural curricula and their implementation in higher education. These are also the central questions surrounding the control of cultural capital. To Scott, political correctness draws serious attention to the institutional structures of inequality that produce racism, sexism, and other forms of discrimination. She argues that political correctness has provided opportunities for minorities, for example, not simply to assimilate to prevailing standards and accept as universal norms what had not previously been their own, but to have the opportunity to question the notion of universality and insist that minority views be taken into account. Henry (1993) provides the counterargument as he labels political correctness as simply a way to respond to the normative rights of groups rather than the rights of individuals. He says it has to do with whatever might be deemed offensive by a member of the perceived rights of that group. Whether challenging the "Dead White Male" Western canon, affirmative action, freedom of expression, or the party line, political correctness, argues Henry, has simply been a vehicle to attack those who have achieved through traditional routes and processes (also see Beckwith and Bauman, 1993; Aufderheide, 1992).

An issue of control over cultural capital hit the Smithsonian Institution and the Air and Space Museum in Washington, D.C., in 1994 and 1995. The issue centered on the exhibit of the Enola Gay, the plane from which the atomic bomb was dropped on Nagasaki and Hiroshima, Japan, to end the Second World War in the Pacific. The Smithsonian was charged, primarily by the American Legion, for designing the exhibit to show the United States as the immoral aggressor rather than as having taken action to end the war and thereby save the lives of hundreds of thousands of North American soldiers who would have died if the war had been permitted to continue. Historians and religious and peace groups had argued that the bombing was not necessary to bring about Japan's surrender. The American Legion and the museum were able to negotiate some of their differences, but ultimately they disagreed on the number of American lives that would have died in an invasion of Japan. With pressures coming from Congress and the White House, the Smithsonian scaled back the exhibit and eliminated all descriptions and explanations associated with the bombing. Historians called it a capitulation to political pressure and an example of historical cleansing akin to the McCarthy era (DeWitt, 1995).

Another example of a struggle to control cultural capital and political correctness is seen in the efforts by the U.S. Department of Education and the National Endowment for the Humanities in the mid-1990s, under Lynne Cheney, to prepare voluntary guidelines for the teaching of world history and American history. The results of the world history efforts suggested the need for a commitment to go beyond Western civilization to include attention to such non-European countries and regions as China, Southeast Asia, Africa, and Central America. The guidelines also called for more analysis and explanation of historical movements and less on rote memorization. Critics argued that the world history guidelines took much attention away from the Western tradition, vilified the United States, and gave too much to the development of the larger world (Thomas, 1994). The American history curriculum was criticized by Cheney and others for giving in to political correctness by devoting too much time to minority ethnic groups at the expense of the country's unique national character. It was also criticized for the inclusion of certain student assignments judged to be biased. One argument was that emphasizing minority contributions to the development of the nation is too divisive and fails to concentrate sufficiently on common, unifying values and political ideals (Coughlin, 1992). Another was that historians seem to concentrate their efforts on everything that is nonwhite, nonWestern, and nonmale, while criticizing the rest. There was considerable lobbying evident with the new Republican majority in Congress early in 1995 to eliminate the American history guidelines and reduce funding for the National Endowment for the Humanities as a result of its sponsorship of the world history effort (Jones, 1995).

Another example of the controversy over diversity in the curriculum surrounded by the issues of political correctness and access to cultural capital came from a conflict over the application of accreditation standards by the Western Association of Schools and Colleges in 1994. The guidelines promulgated by a large majority of member institutions of the association indicated that an appreciation for diversity should be an outcome of undergraduate education and suggested ways that curricula and related campus experiences might be tailored to facilitate racial harmony and cultural sensitivity. Representatives from a relatively small but powerful group of institutions, including Stanford, Cal Tech, and the University of Southern California, among others, protested the new guidelines as an intrusion on academic freedom and an example of how outside agencies were moving toward dictating what and how students should be taught. They also argued that accreditation should reflect the achievement of minimum standards, not the imposition of programs like diversity and multiculturalism (Frammolino, 1994).

The Nation's Political Climate and the Tensions among and between Groups

While political correctness is an example of the tensions surrounding access and control over cultural capital, there are other examples of conflict between and among groups, especially in educational institutions which influence the climate for ethnic studies and multiculturalism. Altbach (1991), in his review of the issues of greatest prominence on college campuses in the 1980s, for example, contends that most student activism was related to racial issues. The greatest catalyst for this activism was South Africa and the demand for universities to eliminate from their investment portfolios stocks of companies doing business in South Africa. A second was the reaction to racial incidents which occurred on campus, and the third was curricular reform or demands to increase multicultural content. Altbach argues the correspondence principle in analyzing the relationship between racial incidents on campus and what occurred in the wider society. He attributes much to the atmosphere created during the Reagan years, including the lack of vigorous enforcement of civil rights laws, the harnessing of the United States Civil Rights Commission, official opposition to new anti-bias initiatives, and the similar attitudes and values of the individuals whom Reagan appointed to provide leadership in the area of minority affairs.

Evidence supporting Altbach's observation can be seen in the attitudes held by differing ethnic and racial groups in the 1990s in the United States. In an article by Karen Winkler (1991), reporting on what some sociologists say is a persistence of racism in the United States, she cites a twenty-year longitudinal study of Blacks and whites in California which shows that whites tend to be more positive about the progress achieved toward racial harmony than are Blacks. Blacks, for example, are likely to express concern over the built-in power and status difference between the races that can be seen in society's institutions. They also argue, for example, that institutional racism and oppression on campus leads them to separate themselves—into different dorms, student centers, tutorial programs, special student newspaper columns, dances, and social clubs—to seek greater independence and potentially greater control over university policies which determine their on-campus behavior.

This perception of a general tension between and among groups was reinforced through two national surveys concerning intergroup relations. The first (Lawrence, 1994) was conducted by the Times Mirror Center for the People and the Press. It found, among others, that attitudes toward minorities, immigrants, and the poor all hardened during the seven years of the survey. Further, for the first time, a majority (51 percent) of the whites agreed with the statement that equal rights for racial minorities had been pushed too far, up from 42 percent two years earlier. The other survey, conducted by the National Conference of Christians and Jews (1994), asked a national sample of respondents to indicate their agreement with a number of positive and negative attributes commonly ascribed to members of ethnic groups in the United States. One of the most striking results of the survey was the differing perceptions held by whites in comparison with other groups. White people were perceived by minorities as bigoted, bossy, and unwilling to share power and wealth, whereas whites held a generally favorable perception of how members of minority groups were faring. Again, one could interpret this finding as evidence of a struggle over cultural capital. Accompanying this distinction was a resounding perception of members of minority groups that they lack the same opportunities held by whites, while whites expressed hostility toward affirmative action policies. Interestingly, while whites and Blacks differed along these status and opportunity lines, it was the minority populations who held most of the negative stereotypes about each other.

Apart from, or as an extension of the struggle among and between groups for access to greater status in society, there are other connections which can be made in the 1990s to provide insight into the trends and issues shaping ethnic studies and multicultural programs. Following the November 1994 national congressional election, for example, the complexion of national politics changed rather dramatically from moderate to conservative. This congressional election, which resulted in members of the Republican party replacing what had been the Democratic majority and becoming the dominant party in both the U. S. Senate and the House of Representatives, meant that the composition of House and Senate committees and their leadership changed the balance of power from more liberal to more conservative. Thus, the early 1990s tension between the Democratically controlled White House and the Republican minority in Congress shifted in 1994 to one that reflected the checks and balances between the executive and legislative branches of government when they are controlled by different political parties.

Following the November 1994 election, the Republicans announced their intention, for example, in the area of education, to cut student grants and work-study programs while increasing the cost of student loans, to implement school voucher programs, to limit money for special education programs, and to make renewed efforts to bring prayer into America's schools, all as part of a more conservative social and political platform. Further, they proposed reductions in support of the arts and humanities and in educational and cultural exchange programs and to eliminate various grant programs in the Department of Education. While such actions did not in themselves determine the course of primary, secondary, and higher education curricula or programs, they clearly supported a conservative political climate and competed with more liberal views. They also made it more difficult financially to achieve goals which involve ethnicity and multiculturalism. Because of the new-found power of the Republicans in Congress, there was an almost immediate reaction in the White House to re-grasp the leadership by moving to enact more conservative policies as well. This action served to temper the traditional inclination of Democrats to increase access and support for diverse populations seeking educational opportunities. Democrats have traditionally argued to limit school vouchers because of an inherent bias in favor of middle- and upper-class students and the likelihood of increasing ethnic and racial segregation. They also have supported making special efforts to attend to those with disabilities and special needs and to maintaining a stricter line between church and state in educational programs (Rosenbaum et. al., 1994).

The Courts, Speech Codes, and Limiting Assistance to Specific Minority Groups

Beyond the 1994 national elections and their impact on the climate for ethnic studies and multiculturalism, another national-level influence shaping the context for such programs came from the courts. A good place to see this influence is in both the First Amendment and the implications for the implementation of campus speech codes and minority student admissions and in student aid and fellowship programs. In the area of speech codes, university campuses are challenged by the extent to which obnoxious, erroneous, and offensive speech should be regulated. And in the area of admissions and financial aid, the issue is the extent to which special efforts can be made to assist members of minority populations to redress past discriminatory treatment.

With regard to speech codes, the question is whether fostering nonoffensive speech is best dealt with through education and example or through rules and regulations. Can universities regulate speech without violating their own reason for existence? In other words, can liberal education proceed to challenge unpopular ideas and rhetoric if speech is limited? Such questions have been dealt with in various ways in the courts and on campuses. The courts have chosen to deal with the First Amendment issue by distinguishing between basically unpopular speech and that speech which is likely to prompt violence, what has been termed "fighting words." While such a ruling still leaves considerable vagueness in defining "fighting words," it leaves intact the right to speak even if it offends civility and community. Under the present doctrine, speech needs to cause an immediate breach of peace—a provocative personal insult that is addressed to an individual, in person, and is intended to cause an immediate violent reaction. On campuses, this means that rules against using abusive language that merely annoys other students, the kind that has often been included in speech codes, will be found unconstitutional.

Prior to the Court's ruling in the early 1990s, several universities had taken steps in regulating speech on campus. The University of Michigan and the University of Wisconsin, among as many as one hundred others, for example, each had in place a process to discipline individuals who demeaned, stigmatized, or victimized another on the basis of, among others, gender, race, age, ethnicity, handicap, or sexual orientation, or who created an intimidating, hostile, or demeaning environment. Benno Schmidt (1991) argued that such policies served to preserve the sense of community on campus but dealt a great blow to freedom of thought and expression. Such policies were typically thrown out as they were tested and found unconstitutional by the courts.

Some of the concerns with free speech have influenced other areas of behavior. For example, following the Clarence Thomas Supreme Court confirmation hearing before Congress, and specifically the charges of sexual harassment by his former colleague Anita Hill, there has been increased attention to gender relations on and off campuses. The courts and the Equal Employment Opportunity Commission in the mid-1990s had still interpreted Title VII of the Civil Rights Act of 1964 and its provision regarding the creation of a "hostile or offensive work environment" for women as requiring only that an individual interpret for herself whether she has been offended by the conduct in question. A University of Michigan sophomore, for example, was threatened with sexual harassment charges after he submitted an essay for his political science class that contained examples using the characters "Dave Stud" and "Joe Sixpack." The professor found the essay inappropriate and offensive. The student reportedly dropped the course. At the University of Pennsylvania, freshman Eden Jacobowitz was accused of racial harassment and threatened with suspension after shouting the equivalent of "Shut up, you water buffalo" to five African-American sorority sisters who were yelling outside his window around midnight. Jacobowitz stated that the phrase, a literal translation of the Hebrew, was slang for "fool" or "dummy" and was not meant to be a racist comment. Nevertheless, the University administration charged him under the school's hate-speech policy. Eventually the charges were dropped and Penn eliminated its speech code (Will, 1993).

George Will (1993), in his weekly *Newsweek* column, decried such attacks on freedom of speech. He cited several other incidents on college campuses which he found disturbing. He reported that at Penn, a group of African American students who were offended by a conservative columnist in the student newspaper met the delivery truck and dumped fourteen thousand copies of the newspaper in the trash. At Penn State and Dartmouth he reported that there were other incidents of conservative newspapers being destroyed because Blacks, feminists, and other special interest and ethnic groups were asserting their assumed right not to be annoyed or to have their feelings hurt by the words expressed by others. He also cited instances where students were punished for making assertions about others. In back-to-back cases in Southern California, for example, a student editor at UCLA was suspended for publishing a cartoon making fun of affirmative action. This was followed by the editor of the student newspaper at nearby California State University, Northridge, being disciplined for criticizing the action taken by the UCLA administration. Will claims that campuses were being monitored in the early 1990s by groups of on-campus students and faculty who were on the look-out for those who were being offended by others, including professors, students, and staff inside and outside of formal courses of instruction.

In a related area of speech-code regulation, this one concerning computer access to pornographic material, college campuses in the mid-1990s were faced with the issue of censorship of cyberspace through the Internet or global computer network. The case which focused this debate occurred at Carnegie Mellon University in Pittsburgh, a national leader in computer-related studies. The university blocked access to bulletin boards that students could use to call up sexually explicit written material and pictures through the international computer network. A student rally caused the university to back down on the written material but it maintained the ban on the photography. The legal issues are complex, argued CMU, as the state of Pennsylvania can prosecute the university for allowing access to pornographic material by those less than eighteen years of age and under federal law the sending of obscene pictures across state lines is prohibited. Further, using local community standards to judge what cyberspace material is obscene is extremely difficult. Because cyberspace has no particular community which it can call home, it is not clear which, if any, local community standards would apply. Perhaps to fill this void, the United States Congress began hearings on the issue in the spring of 1995.

Another area, beyond speech codes, where the courts have established guidelines influencing racial and ethnic relations is in college admissions. The recent activity in this area builds on a case in the 1970s when a white, male applicant, Alan Bakke, was denied admission to the medical school at the University of California. Bakke filed suit against the University and argued that other students, Hispanic and Black, were admitted instead of him even though his record of academic achievement and standardized admission test scores were superior to theirs. He accurately indicated that the minority students were accepted through a special admissions policy which set aside sixteen places for Black and Hispanic students, thereby placing at a disadvantage other students whose qualifications for admission were higher. In 1976, the California Supreme Court ruled in favor of Bakke and admitted him to the university. The case was appealed by the University but the original decision was generally upheld as the United States Supreme Court decided that universities could consider, but not rely exclusively, on race in determining admissions eligibility. The decision was perceived as an extension of the principles underlying affirmative action, or actions intended to rectify the effects of past discrimination. The results of the Bakke litigation have not been satisfactory to either higher education institutions or to those who desire greater higher education access among racial and ethnic groups. The effect, however, has been to challenge the practice of using race or ethnicity in such decisions, as such an approach uses traits and characteristics over which the individual has little control, in addition to achievement, as a means to gain some form of immediate privilege.

Based on the Bakke decision, the consideration of race and ethnicity has also been employed in making decisions regarding the granting of fellowship and student financial aid. This issue was challenged in the fall of 1994 by the United States Court of Appeals, Fourth Circuit, in the state of Maryland. A Hispanic student, Daniel Podberesky, was denied a scholarship at the University of Maryland because the scholarship was available only to African American students and thus Podberesky was unable to compete. The university argued that thirty scholarships annually for African Americans because it was unable to attract such students and it needed to take extraordinary action to overcome its negative image among African Americans to ensure their increased access and success. The appeals court, however, said that race could be used as a basis for such policies only if it could be shown that the policies were remedial for some specific effects of past discrimination by the university. The conclusion reached by the court, however, indicated that the university was taking steps at racial balancing rather than tailoring efforts to provide a remedy for specific conditions. The court opined that there was insufficient evidence to indicate that the university's actions had led to lower minority enrollment, retention, or graduation rates and that these outcomes could be explained by factors other than past actions by the university (Jaschik, 1994). This court action followed another in the state of Texas where a federal judge ruled that the University of Texas Law School could not maintain separate admissions programs for whites and minorities.

Affirmative Action and California Referenda

To some observers in higher education, affirmative action programs in the mid-1990s came under additional scrutiny at the state and national levels primarily because of the growing backlash by white males (see, for example, Dziech, 1995). Demographics indicated that it was the white male sector of the population which was responsible for putting the more conservative Republican majority in the Congress in the fall of 1994. One factor associated with the white male vote was federal policy designed to increase the efficacy of minority-owned businesses and industries, a policy which the United States Supreme Court ruled against in the spring of 1995. Another reason white males have become more alienated by affirmative action programs is said to be admissions, financial assistance, and related programs in higher education favoring one or more student minority interest group over another. This backlash led the Regents of the University of California to vote to end racial preferences in admissions and hiring throughout the UC system. Dziech explains it is the white male who receives no special assistance, yet it is also him who is expected to pay for the transgressions of early generations.

A case which has further alienated white males involved a female student who wanted to be admitted to the Citadel, an all male college. The courts held that the applicant, Shannon R. Faulkner, should be admitted into the corps of cadets at the public military college in South Carolina. The question is of interest here because of its ultimate impact on the separate-but-equal provisions for educational programs. Faulkner was first denied admission and then permitted to attend the university as a day student, but she was barred from leadership training through extracurricular programs. It was her lack of access to such programs that she argued was preventing her from receiving equal treatment (Manegold, 1995). Ultimately, the college admitted her but she withdrew in her first semester due in part to the demanding physical fitness regimen of the program.

The outcome of the recent court cases concerning admissions and financial assistance mentioned above, while not yet definitive, along with the thesis regarding the alienation of white males casts other conservative rings in the arena of race and ethnic relations. The issue of using race and ethnicity as a partial basis for admissions or financial aid continues to draw national attention. This is especially the case in California as voters in the late 1990s will vote on a proposed constitutional amendment, known as the California Civil Rights Initiative, which would prohibit the use of race, sex, color, ethnicity, or national origin as a criterion for positive or negative discrimination in any of the state's public employment, public education, or public contracting venues. Some fear that the passage of such a measure on the California ballot would assist in placing a similar amendment to the U.S. Constitution, mandating a race- and ethnicity-free public policy. Such efforts can once again be interpreted as casting a negative view over programs, like ethnic and multicultural studies, which use as their base the cultural characteristics of particular segments of the population.

One reason for the anxiety expressed nationally over the impact of the impending nondiscrimination policy is what California voters did in November 1994 as they voted overwhelmingly to pass Proposition 187. It again reflects the tensions and conflict-oriented climate associated with race and ethnic relations in the United States in the 1990s. Proposition 187 rendered all undocumented aliens ineligible for any welfare services, schooling, and nonemergency medical care while requiring teachers and doctors to report to state agencies and the Immigration and Naturalization Service those they suspected of living in California illegally. In addition, the sale of false documents became a state felony. Even though there were numerous law suits filed immediately after the passage of the measure, and even though there will be many years of litigation before its ultimate fate is known, the passage of the measure is itself a reflection of the concerns of the larger society. Unfortunately, the impact of the measure on California's minority population is complicated and uneven. Kenneth Noble (1994), for example, reports the following anomaly. He notes that the proposition calls for expelling from school the teen-age child of undocumented workers. The child may have grown up in the United States, learned English, and know little of his or her native country. The proposition says little, however, about the child who grows up in a mixed-status household: for example, one in which the father's residence was legalized under the 1986 federal amnesty law, the mother is newly arrived and undocumented, and an infant is born a United States citizen.

In an editorial written by William J. Bennett, former Secretary of Education in the Reagan administration (1994), appearing in the *Washington Post* a month after the passage of Proposition 187, he noted that some prominent conservatives were looking to pass similar legislation in other states and calling for a national moratorium on legal immigration (see, for example, Buckley, 1994). Interestingly, however, the politically conservative Bennett argued that such actions would be inappropriate and called Proposition 187 "shortsighted" in that it threw school children onto the streets, and "anticonservative" in that it called on private citizens to report to authorities those suspected to be illegal aliens. While acknowledging the serious problems posed by illegal immigration, Bennett argued that this concern should not be transmitted to the legal immigrant community. He pointed out, for example, that the legal immigrant is characterized as industrious, hard working, and self reliant; as holding strong family values and an allegiance to religious faith; and as having made numerous contributions to the wider society in the sciences and in the information technology fields. He also pointed out that immigration does not cause higher unemployment rates among nonimmigrant workers and that except for refugees, immigrants receive less welfare and are a huge net contributor to both Social Security and annual government levied taxes. He also cites a study indicating that immigrants are less likely to engage in criminal activity.

The Relation Between Genes and the Environment on IQ

Bennett's editorial shows how one issue, in this case illegal immigrants in California, spills over onto other issues like immigrants in general. The lack of clear boundaries around such issues is suggestive of the ways in which race and cultural concerns get muddled and lead to stereotypical responses with intended and unintended consequences. Another example of such issues concerns the nature and nurture argument surrounding intelligence and, to some extent, other physical and mental capabilities of humans.

A book published by social scientists Charles Murray and Richard J. Herrnstein in 1994 fueled this episodic controversy through an analysis of IQ scores among Blacks and Whites. They argue that in the United States during recent decades, cognitive ability (as measured by standardized test scores) rather than level of schooling, religion, social class, and so on, has become the route to social mobility and achievement. Further, they indicate that those with IQs of over 115 are becoming more separated and isolated from those who score lower and that this is feeding a social stratification system based on intelligence. The authors' argument was about the hereditability of intelligence, pointing out that black school children perform more poorly on IQ tests than do white children. They infer that because IQ scores of children correlate highly with those of their parents, IQ must be influenced, at least in part, by genes. They report that around 60 percent of the explanation for low IQ could be explained by genetic factors.

Murray and Herrnstein, in reviewing the literature in this area, align themselves with the more classical definition of intelligence, that is, one based on an assumption that mental ability is associated with a person's knowledge, behaviors, and skills and can be measured by standardized IQ tests. By adopting this approach, they eschew alternatives whereby intelligence is either associated with the processes used to apply information for problem solving or with peoples' abilities to solve real-life problems and create new and effective ways to deal with them. In both of these latter alternatives, traditional IQ tests are judged as inappropriate ways to measure such abilities.

Traditionally, it is common for nongenetic explanations to be tossed into the nature-nurture discussion, including the cultural bias of testing, poverty and socioeconomic status, racism, and so on. Such alternative arguments are typically grounded in assumptions about either the ways in which different segments of society prepare or do not prepare their offspring for the demands of other segments, or the ways in which one segment purposely works against the equal treatment and access to society's resources of another segment. Thus, some argue that lack of access to prenatal care among many African Americans, for example, is more likely to result in low-birth-weight babies with negative consequences for subsequent physical and cognitive growth and development. Such impact may have little to do with genetic make-up. Further, such deficits in the newly born can be impacted through nutrition programs, early educational programs, and changes in the social environment to which a young child is exposed. Head Start programs involving pre-school-age children and one or more parent, for example, constitute one example of an intervention effort which has demonstrated positive effects on school achievement. Murray and Herrnstein are adept at explaining away such alternative explanations while also admitting that there is no totally scientific way of determining what proportion of the difference in IQ is due to genes.

As with the leap from illegal to legal immigrants discussed by Bennett, the extrapolation done with genetic claims regarding the basis for cognitive ability can be generalized much beyond any reasonable reference point. This is because, for example, cognitive ability can be associated with a host of other variables, including poverty, unemployment, dropping out of school, criminal activity, out-of-wedlock births, and so on. Further, if genes are so dominant in explaining cognitive ability, it would be nearly worthless to pursue educational and related intervention strategies to counter such influences. The genetic view in the genetic versus the environment or nature/nurture issue is an old one which, as suggested above, re-emerges every so often without any certainty as to the validity of its assertions, many of which are as likely to be reflective of racism as they are of the scientific value of their analysis (Morin, 1995).

The Politics and Agenda of the Religious Right

An important part of cultural behavior is the way in which beliefs are codified and manifested in religious organizations and thus reflected in one's identity and group affiliation. As we know, religion can also be the basis for social, political, and economic action as belief systems become the basis for establishing a vision for institutions, communities, and the nation as a whole. While there are numerous religious organizations in the United States which have demonstrated their power and influence over local and national policies, as with more conservative Roman Catholics and their stand against abortion, only the religious right in the 1990s has achieved a critical mass sufficient to influence local and national policy. Like other special interests, it is the intention of these religious conservatives to see that standards of behavior reflect their shared beliefs and cultural philosophy, one that is typically antagonistic to pluralism and church/state separation. They have done so through the media as well as through making community-based efforts to have their members appointed or elected to policymaking boards governing schools and other public institutions. The movement has taken on particular issues, like school prayer, civil rights for gays and lesbians, abortion, school choice, and school curricula, with special interest. Composed mostly of Protestants, usually evangelical or fundamental in orientation, affiliates are said to have increased by two or possibly three times in the last several years. Pat Robertson and his "Christian Coalition" and James Dobson's "Focus on the Family" are among the larger organizations who identify with the religious conservatives. Both have taken an interest in what gets published and purchased by schools and placed in classrooms or on library shelves. An interesting case in this area occurred in 1991 when a student council in a publicly supported state institution, the University of Virginia, turned down a request for financial support of a Christian student organization that wished to publish a magazine intended to discuss "biblical Christianity." The case was complicated because it was both a free speech issue as well as a separation of church and state issue (Greenhouse, 1994). In 1995, the United States Supreme

Court ruled that the state university had to subsidize student-run religious publications if it gave other student publications financial support.

One of the targets of the religious right, and another area of tension in the country, concerns the rights of gays and lesbians. In spring 1994 there were at least ten states in which conservative groups were pushing for ballot initiatives to limit gay-rights laws or strip gay-rights organizations of public funding. Included as some of the particular issues drawing attention are books by gay authors or courses that discuss homosexuality in any way other than as abnormal and destructive, spousal benefits for same-sex couples, and antidiscrimination rules toward gays and lesbians on higher education campuses. Faculty members who have been teaching courses in which sexual orientation constitutes a segment are threatened by such initiatives and claim they are an encroachment on academic freedom. Such controversies also spill over into the student body as gay and lesbian organizations on campuses become the targets for verbal, if not physical, abuse. Furthermore, such initiatives have caused gays and lesbians to mobilize efforts to confront the antagonists, which in turn has caused some campuses to become polarized around sexual orientation issues (Carmona, 1994).

Conclusion

It is not surprising that those seeking to institute ethnic studies or multi-culturalism programs on college and university campuses are perplexed by how to respond to some of the conservative trends and concerns they see being expressed in the wider society and within which they must pursue their goals. To think that higher education must wade through this myriad of issues, all current and contemporary, is mind-boggling for the administrator and certainly estab-lishes constraints on the advocates of changing the intergroup-relations climate and educational agenda. As the foregoing discussion suggests, challenging the dominant group as an advocate of a modified curriculum from inside or outside of higher education institutions is often interwoven with other intergroup-relations issues, including demographic shifts, control over what knowledge is of most worth, the political climate at the national and local levels, the courts, and special interest groups like the religious right. There is also the backlash from ethnic studies and multicultural efforts, which are labeled divisive rather than inclusive. Given these concerns, it is no wonder that faculty, staff, and students become interested and concerned, and sometimes polarized, about the perspectives and values that ethnic studies and multiculturalism represent.

As we have indicated in earlier chapters, the basic issue underlying the conflict is whether emphasis should be placed on the similarities among and between groups rather than on cultural differences. In effect, will the nation survive over the long term if separate groups are permitted to have their background and traditions form part of the mosaic of the higher education agenda? Thus, ethnic studies, and to a somewhat lesser extent multiculturalism, require some level of acceptance that racial and ethnic identity is a positive, individual choice to be made by each individual, and that groups have a right to see their particular histories and lifeways reflected in the broad parameters of higher education curricula. To achieve such ends given the counter pressures, will depend on faculty, students, and community interest groups influencing each other, as well as the boards which govern and the administrators who lead the institutions which they have targeted for change. On the assumption that the correspondence principle explains both the primarily dominant-group influence on campus issues, as well as the challenges to them, and furthermore that most individuals who serve on the faculty, on boards, or as campus administrators are affiliated in some ways with such dominant groups, they are often perceived as part of the problem as well as part of the solution.

Today, many campuses continue to be faced with the question of which orientation to take with regard to intergroup relations. If they do nothing, they will be criticized for, among other things, not providing the preparation needed by students to enter the diverse linguistic and cultural world of which they now are a part. If they move toward ethnic studies, they must confront the issues associated with the questions of academic legitimacy, organizational status, and the like, as well as signal all other ethnic groups as to whether they can also aspire to similar treatment. And if they decide to implement multicultural studies, arguments associated with political correctness will emerge. Further, those lobbying for ethnic studies will argue that the curriculum will be too shallow, not do justice to the critical contribution made to the larger society by a respective ethnic group, be poorly articulated and organized across disciplinary lines, and be dependent on too many faculty, many of whom will at least initially be ill-prepared to teach the revised content.

Assuming that the goal is to prepare students for a multicultural community, either as having been liberally educated or to act as professionals in practice, there is little likelihood that the first option—defending the status quo—is viable. In the latter two instances—whether to pursue ethnic studies or multicultural studies—there is little reason to pit one against the other. Instead, they should be perceived as complementary, providing both the interdisciplinary and cross-cultural focus as well an in-depth treatment of one or more identifiable groups. The means for choosing which groups around which to build a critical mass of students and faculty should be decided based on enrollment, demographic trends, or local community and regional history and tradition. Thus, while the larger society places constraints on what institutions might do, the institution itself must come to terms with the vision of what kind of linguistic abilities, intergroup-relations skills, and knowledge of the history and culture of various population segments, needs to be acquired by students to enable them to participate as potentially highly mobile citizens of the world.

Institutions, like individuals, need to develop an identity in the intergroup-relations arena, an identity which comes to terms with the institution's collective values, its community, its demography, its nature as a teaching and/or research institution, its goals for students, and so on. It must create this identity on its own, but in concert with the social and political constraints on its history and its current existence. It need not be an identity that is never changing; it will change as opposing forces provide for new problem solving. To bring together the forces of a campus, however, is no easy feat. Evidence suggests that faculty often see little urgency about diversity issues, while students and their respective student affairs administrators in the institution carry on the major dialogue about diversity issues. This helps explain why it is the extracurriculum rather than the regular curriculum that is often the focus of diversity issues. When faculty are engaged, they are less likely to make efforts to integrate diversity issues into their coursework, instead being satisfied with the relegation of responsibility to ethnic, gender, and racial studies or to the general education requirements (Levine, 1991).

All of this suggests that relative to intergroup relations, the higher education institution is not very well organized or structured and there is little tradition to support a commitment to either multiculturalism or ethnic studies. Colleges and departments are often compartmentalized and hierarchically ordered, and often do not place value on content which is not central to the discipline. Further, communication across department and college lines is often limited and seldom engages faculty or students in substantive scholarship, teaching, and learning. Given such conditions, it is clear why more attention is often placed on recruiting and supporting faculty and students, actions which are less likely to alter the way in which the educational institution conducts its business as opposed to, for example, transforming the curriculum, a task which requires an intellectual commitment.

CHAPTER 6

Alternatives to Multicultural and Ethnic Studies: Strategies for Change

In the preceding chapters, we have discussed the development and status of ethnic studies and multiculturalism in United States colleges and universities. Chapter 5 reviewed the conservative challenge of the 1990s and related institutional constraints on enhancing multiculturalism and ethnic studies in higher education. We now turn to the question: How do colleges and universities best prepare students for common citizenship in a diverse, democratic state while also nurturing group cultures, values, and institutional participation? In practice, to answer this question means melding the specific, but powerful, focus of ethnic studies with the broader, but sometimes contentious, vision of multi- culturalism. Attention to the institutional culture and extracurricular activities are additional vital elements in this effort.

Ethnic studies has been one component of fostering diversity in higher education over the last several decades. We have seen how ethnic studies programs arose as higher education enrollment expanded dramatically after World War II, as minority enrollment grew in the 1960s and 1970s, and as the success and spirit of the Civil Rights movement promoted diversity and empowered previously underrepresented groups.

Like multiculturalism, ethnic-specific programs assume that society is segmented into groups, that the higher education curriculum should reflect society's diversity, that the interdisciplinary study offered by ethnic studies benefits a broader realm of scholarship, and that in a democracy groups have rights to a share in societal and institutional power. However, there are limits to the contribution that ethnic studies can make to fostering diversity throughout higher education institutions. For the most part, ethnic studies' most ardent supporters promote them to fulfill limited group interests rather than to increase all students' exposure to diversity. As a result, ethnic studies programs have frequently had to clarify whether they owe their existence to a definite knowledge base or to political power, have struggled for departmental status, and have endured criticism that they contribute to divisiveness and isolate ethnic group students. At the same time, because they are often marginalized units within universities, ethnic studies programs have limited ability to nurture group cultures, values, and institutional participation. As a result, they have had to balance their growing acceptance on campuses with loss of ties to, and support from, their ethnic communities, while also carrying on internal debates about focus and subject matter. Concerned with their own direction and survival, they have not had the resources or influence to reach into many areas of the curriculum or campus life.

Multiculturalism has represented a broader set of developments, movements, and points of view related to an assumption that today's students will live and work in increasingly diverse environments and to a radical critique of societal and educational power relations. Various campus issues are tied to multiculturalism, including the debate that pits individual rights for free speech against group rights for protection from stereotyping and abuse. Even more than ethnic studies, multiculturalism has been at the center of a loud and contentious public debate in the 1990s. The debate has focused on what students should study in college, who should decide what they should learn, and whether changes in what they study threatens higher education institutions. As we saw in chapter 5, the debate relates to the control of cultural capital, and its intensity reflects the changing political climate and tension between groups.

In practice, multiculturalism has tended to focus in depth on a few departments in the humanities and social sciences, on their related professional organizations, on the content of their disciplines, and on a few general requirements for all students, such as first-year literature or introductory history courses. While the public debate has often been triggered by proposed revisions in general requirements (the "canon"), many students remain largely unaffected by the multiculturalism debate, just as they receive little or no exposure to ethnic studies programs. Students in the sciences or engineering, once they are beyond introductory literature or composition courses, study in an environment where ethnic studies and multicultural issues are rarely, if ever, encountered.

Ethnic studies and multiculturalism as currently conceived bring certain strengths to achieving the dual goals of preparing students for a more diverse society while nurturing subordinate group values, culture, and institutional participation. However, each also brings important constraints. In this chapter we review some of these constraints, discuss the imperatives for continuing to seek diversity and group participation, outline a number of possible models for changes that would help to achieve these dual goals, and discuss particular contributions extracurricular activities and campus culture might make in promoting diversity while preserving group identity. As we proceed, two issues should be kept in mind.

- In many institutions, ethnic studies and multiculturalism are not mutually supportive.

For some supporters of ethnic studies, multiculturalism looms as a new threat to these programs' well-being and existence. They see general diversity requirements and efforts by disciplines and departments to hire more minority faculty or to offer more individual ethnic studies courses as potential excuses for cuts in their programs, faculty, and resources. For other supporters of ethnic studies, multiculturalism lacks the sharp critique of society that they feel ethnic studies delivers. San Juan (1991), for example, maintains that multiculturalism as practiced by traditional institutions usually excludes concepts of dominant and subordinate cultures by promoting tolerance of diverse ethnic practices. In this view, racism is reduced to a matter of ideas or attitudes that can be changed through education or acculturation. However, this critique of multiculturalism mistakenly denies its economic, political, and behavioral content and ignores those proponents of multiculturalism who raise basic questions about the relationship among groups. In some institutions, specific approaches and interests of those who promote multiculturalism may not be those of most interest or relevance to an ethnic studies program and its constituency. Likewise, those who support multicultural and ethnic studies initiatives may have very different bases within the university. In some cases, ethnic studies proponents are working to establish or maintain a department, center, or program. Multicultural efforts tend to focus on the approach of an established department or on university-wide core requirements.

- Diversity and the preservation of group identity and position are major issues at most colleges and universities, but multicultural efforts and ethnic studies are far from universal in higher education in the United States.

Multiculturalism has received a great deal of publicity in the 1990s, and ethnic studies are once again growing in higher education (Magner, 1991). However, the publicity generated by the controversial aspects of these efforts and programs leads to the mistaken impression that they are nearly universal. In one of the few studies of the status of multiculturalism and ethnic studies on college campuses, Levine and Cureton (1992) surveyed 270 colleges and universities in the United States, stratified by Carnegie-type, in 1991. Levine and Cureton found that only about one-third of the institutions have some kind of a general multicultural requirement. Moreover, these requirements vary widely in content and structure. Most (68 percent) are distribution requirements; only 12 percent focus on domestic diversity. Moreover, while one-third or more of the institutions offer course(s) in African American (43 percent), Asian American (35 percent), or Hispanic American (37 percent) studies, no more than 10 percent offer programs or departments in these areas. Levine and Cureton conclude that while multicultural efforts are widespread, they are far from universal. They are also largely add-ons to existing practice and are limited in their effect on the historic content of what has been taught in higher education.

We move on to examine some of the constraints to achieving the dual goals of preparation for diversity and promotion of group culture and participation.

Constraints to Increasing Ethnic and Multicultural Studies

In addition to facing the pressures from the dominant (and increasingly conservative) groups detailed in chapter 5, colleges and universities confront a number of constraints as they attempt to increase ethnic and multicultural studies. These constraints include generic difficulties associated with institutional change, conflicts between ethnic studies and multicultural initiatives, and conservative opposition to the promotion of diversity and to the special recognition or study of subordinate groups. They are similar to what Takaki (1993) lists as barriers to group studies:

- Budget cuts, which mean traditional departments guard their resources
- Opposition based on preserving power and privilege
- Conservative attacks, with calls of "political correctness"
- White perplexity over the changing racial composition of United States society
- The sense of some groups that they are losing power and influence

Among the generic constraints to change efforts in higher education is money. Budgetary considerations have often been cited as a reason for not moving ethnic studies programs to departmental status. Programs are less expensive than departments and involve fewer long-term financial commitments in fields where there are few possibilities of sustained outside funding or few prospects of major gifts from constituents. Multicultural programs implemented across the university can also be expensive. Successful programs require extensive time for faculty to consult with experts, to rewrite their own course content, and to plan curricula. In some high profile cases, the potential for public controversies related to changes in the core or to expressions of ethnic or racial conflict can make decision makers nervous and stifle change.

The decision-making process has been another institutional constraint. Higher education has clear hierarchies that determine who can make decisions about curriculum change. The academic culture dictates who should be consulted and to what degree about curricular changes such as the addition of a diversity requirement. In many institutions, changes related to diversity must satisfy many groups, some with little relation to ethnic studies or to disciplines concerned with multiculturalism. Examples given in chapter 3—such as those from the Universities of Texas and Oregon—demonstrate the powerful roles that various constituencies within the university play in creating and blocking change. For example, at the University of Oregon, the multicultural effort became entangled with larger issues of control, including faculty control of the curriculum. A diversity requirement was finally passed only when a new draft was created by a committee that was perceived as being largely mainstream faculty and as not having its own political agenda. At the University of Texas, the eventual defeat of new content for a required composition course began when some English Department faculty launched a media and letter-writing campaign that called the course ideological, racial, biased, and propagandistic. In both cases, strategic political skills by faculty and administrators were required to move the initiatives.

Faculty face very practical constraints on their time in the face of an ever-growing information load (Goldstein, 1994). In many disciplines, the growth of ethnic studies, women's studies, and interdisciplinary, multicultural scholarship has produced a vast amount of new material as well as new concepts and theories. Faculty who wish to bring this information to students must make major commitments of personal time to acquaint themselves with recent research literature and frameworks. An alternative is for institutions to sponsor—at a cost—seminars and other means to help faculty update their syllabi. As a result, changes in curricula have often been piecemeal and add-ons with limited overall impact.

Finally, "turf" issues may constrain the achievement of the goals. Goldstein (1994) argues that an inherent danger exists when a particular department or school is responsible for the cultural diversity program. What he labels as a "strong sense of proprietorship" may discourage other departments from offering courses.

Conflict between multicultural efforts and ethnic studies programs is another major constraint. While seemingly committed to the same general goals, the two approaches have the potential for conflict. In institutions where departments have undertaken multicultural initiatives such as adding courses about ethnic group experiences or hiring faculty of color without collaborative planning or consultation with existing ethnic studies programs, conflicts have sometimes arisen. The marginal nature of ethnic studies programs—some of which may have not achieved departmental status even after fifteen or twenty years of existence in an institution—contributes to the conflict. Often without the ability to hire their own faculty and without the status that identifies them with a specific academic discipline, ethnic studies programs are very concerned about the possibility of their eventual termination. Ethnic studies faculty also worry that if an institution implements large-scale multicultural requirements, they will be called upon to offer service courses to students who have little interest in ethnic studies. They are also concerned that they will be overburdened with inadequately compensated work advising colleagues on curriculum content for other departments.

A further constraint to ethnic and multicultural studies is the growing conservative opposition to the promotion of diversity and the strong opposition to programs for specific groups, whether through multicultural requirements or ethnic studies. Often choices are cast in terms of support for, or attacks on, Western civilization. Yet at heart is power—the power to decide what counts as knowledge, what knowledge should be taught, who does the teaching, and so forth. Auletta and Jones (1990) write that the battle is about who will define and maintain the culture, social relations, and institutions. The conflict is over the control of cultural capital and moves far beyond the university in society-wide issues, such as the recent battles over gay and lesbian rights.

In some institutions, power has been exerted through monetary contributions made to promote a particular point of view. For example, in 1991 Yale University received a $20 million contribution from a Fort Worth family to further Yale's study of Western civilization. The grant was designated to pay for a year-long course to be offered Yale undergraduates that would analyze every major development in Western history and would make a symbolic statement that at Yale, multiculturalism was not laying siege to Western civilization as it was at other colleges and universities. Eleven full-time faculty were to teach the course. Soon after the gift was announced, the Yale president and dean who negotiated the agreement left the university. Remaining on campus were a large group of faculty and students who denied the need for the course and a substantial conservative faculty and student lobby who demanded that the course be offered exactly as stipulated in the gift. The university faced a dilemma. Supporters of the course demanded that it be prepared and taught as earlier specified. Opponents argued that the university already had over 100 undergraduate courses that dealt with Western civilization (Steinberg, 1994). The proposed program had not been implemented by early 1995 and Yale agreed to a request from the family to return the money (Campbell, 1995).

Challenges to diversity and particularly to efforts to ensure that groups' culture and roles are protected have also received support, including financial support, from conservative foundations. For example, in 1993 the William Donner Foundation funded a project, "The Best That Has Been Thought and Said," a curriculum to "expose the ideological bias and hollow pretention of much of what currently passes for multiculturalism" (William Donner Foundation, 1993).

Finally, there are intellectual constraints, with those who support diversity or ethnic studies vulnerable to the accusation of closed-mindedness—the very problem they seek to dispel from their students, but one to which they may be very sensitive. Takaki (1993) describes a critical review of his book *Iron Cages: Race and Culture in Nineteenth Century America* in which he was scolded for "reverse discrimination" because of his description of whites in terms of greed and brutality and his focus on the experience of ethnic groups in the United States and not on even more horrendous experiences of ethnic minorities in other societies.

Countering these constraints to the achievement of the goals of diversity and group identity and participation are a variety of imperatives to change. We examine some of those now.

Imperatives for Change

Although there are constraints to achieving the dual goals of preparing students for diversity and nurturing groups' cultures and their participation in higher education, there are also imperatives for making changes needed to further these goals. Among the imperatives are the continued growth of underserved minority populations and their unfulfilled desire to enter higher education, the diverse experiences of students now in precollegiate education that will lead them to expect more sophisticated materials and teaching about diversity and ethnic groups, the support that foundations and accrediting agencies are providing for new multicultural and ethnic studies efforts, and the belief that universities have a responsibility for assisting in intergroup relations.

Generally, discussions of multiculturalism and ethnic studies emphasize the growing diversity of higher education and the increasing numbers of ethnic minorities, immigrants, women, and older adults who are attending colleges and universities. We have discussed these important trends earlier and here reaffirm that they provide justification for increased attention to diversity in higher education curriculum and culture. At the same time, this positive message about increased access should not obscure the fact that many groups still lag behind the average in participation in higher education. To cite one example, the Hispanic population grew five times as fast as the overall population in the 1980s, but the number of Hispanic college students grew much more slowly: from 384,000 in 1976 to 624,000 in 1986. Moreover, the percentage of Hispanic high school graduates enrolled in college during the same period dropped from 35.8 percent to less than 30 percent. Hispanic students are attending increasingly segregated schools and will come in greater numbers to colleges with preparation for college that does not match that of Asians and whites (Orfield, 1989). Improved and expanded multicultural and ethnic studies programs, as well as attention to the culture of the institution and to the extracurricular context, can benefit these students. In addition, serving these populations has the potential for aiding higher education financially. Orfield predicts a decline in overall higher education enrollment, but suggests this problem could be solved by focusing on underserved populations to keep up overall enrollment. This would involve changing recruitment and retention programs, modifying curriculum, and hiring more faculty from backgrounds similar to those of the students.

A second imperative for preparing students for diversity and increasing group participation is the diverse experiences and expectations of students now in precollegiate education. Colleges and universities will soon have many students who have had elementary and secondary instruction shaped by the growing influence of multiculturalism in precollegiate education. Thus, entire cohorts of students are now entering higher education with backgrounds unlike those of students who graduated from high school in the 1950s, 1960s, or 1970s. Moreover, in some school districts, particularly in urban areas on either coast, students will have attended schools with more diversity than many of the colleges and universities they will attend. In a few districts, the levels of ethnic consciousness and student participation in ethnic studies will also rival those available in higher education institutions. A 1994 PBS documentary showed how Berkeley High School in California is both diverse and highly conscious of this diversity (Public Broadcasting Service, 1994).

Many students soon to enter higher education may also have experience with more sophisticated multicultural curricula based on the guidelines and materials that emerged from national studies and panels convened in the late 1980s and early 1990s. In the case referred to in chapter 5, a panel of historians commissioned by the U.S. Department of Education and the National Endowment for the Humanities during the Bush Administration developed new voluntary standards for the teaching of world history for grades 5–12. The standards add non-European events and people and emphasize pedagogy that teaches students to explain, analyze, and explore historical movements. They move beyond the study of "great civilizations" traditionally considered important to Europe. For example, the guidelines bring in more information about Africa than has usually been taught. New standards for elementary schools will take the same approach. On the state levels, new social studies standards in New York State will stress global studies and the interrelationships between regions of the United States. Teachers will focus on broad patterns and themes with emphasis on the twentieth century (Thomas, 1994). Students educated under these kinds of guidelines and materials will come with broader knowledge, different attitudes, and more sophisticated understandings of ethnicity, diversity, and intergroup relations. In addition, these issues appear to be coming to the forefront of American political debate, raising their visibility among students even further. Early in the campaign, candidates for the 1996 Republican presidential nomination criticized the national standards for American history and voiced opposition to bilingual education and affirmative action (Pitsch, 1995). Higher education will need to provide students with more complete multicultural offerings and new approaches to ethnic studies to keep pace with this increased sophistication.

A third imperative for changes comes from the support that foundations and accrediting agencies are providing for multicultural and ethnic studies efforts. For example, the Ford Foundation has funded efforts in multiculturalism and in women's studies in recent years. Accrediting agencies can play an extremely critical role in change, with institutions devoting large amounts of time and resources preparing for their accreditation reviews. In some cases accreditation agencies have made diversity an expectation for the institutions they review. As indicated in chapter 5, for example, in 1994 the Western Association of Schools and Colleges (which accredits colleges in California, Hawaii, and Guam) approved ethnic diversity guidelines that spelled out the specifics of an ethnic diversity standard adopted in 1988. The guidelines met with opposition from some institutions which felt they were intrusive (Leatherman, 1994). Whether opposed or supportive, the universities will undoubtedly feel pressure to change in response to such directives.

A fourth imperative for change is the expectation among many in society, including many members of ethnic groups, that universities—even when they are conceived as part of the problem or aloof from communities—have a responsibility to assist in intergroup relations. Hayes-Bautista (1992), for example, argues that universities should play a role in developing the intellectual frameworks that explain how ethnic groups are bound together. Hayes-Bautista believes that what holds communities together—what ultimately quelled the riots in Los Angeles—are values and other "glue," citing the values of Latinos and their origin in a larger Latino Catholic tradition. He argues that educated people should understand at least two of these broad traditions. His views on community are but one set of ideas among many that universities will increasingly discuss about intergroup relations.

Related to this expectation that higher education will contribute ideas and concepts related to racial and ethnic groups is the need to clarify the relationship between multiculturalism and ethnic studies. On one hand, multiculturalism has produced what has been called the "cultural wars," the loud, somewhat inward-looking debate about what constitutes the canon. Within this debate have been some of the most radical critiques of what is taught—or not taught—in higher education. On the other hand, multiculturalism has often represented a very broad, generic approach to diversity. In practice, multicultural or diversity requirements have often meant no more than the addition of a few minority or female authors to a syllabus or asking students to take one of a whole array of courses—some with solid intellectual frameworks and some that are merely exotic or unusual—about other cultures. Meanwhile, ethnic studies programs range from highly focused programs with a clear political agenda and or a specific conceptual core such as Afrocentrism, to uncoordinated collections of courses about a particular group, taught in a variety of departments. For the student who wants to understand intergroup relations, including how ethnicity relates to race, social class, or gender, ethnic studies can lack the needed breadth. As we explore models for change, we include several approaches for bringing multicultural and ethnic studies efforts together.

Models for Change

We turn now to various models for achieving the dual goals of preparing students for diversity and the nurturing of group culture, values, and participation. We are particularly interested in how to move beyond the recent debates about the canon and the content of ethnic studies to more effective strategies by which higher education can teach students about intergroup relations. One approach is to strengthen existing programs. Other models include teaching the conflicts, teaching themes rather than groups, and using international or cross-cultural approaches. Below we discuss these alternatives.

Many institutions could strengthen their programs by more clearly focusing existing courses and resources. As noted earlier, recent studies suggest that multiculturalism and ethnic studies are far from universal. In many institutions, the multicultural or diversity requirements accept almost any course that includes material about group differences, ethnicity, or cultural change. Often, the content does not include conceptual frameworks for intergroup relations. For example, general courses about the art, literature, politics, or other elements of a country or region appear to be acceptable as multiculturalism experiences in many institutions. Moreover, the study shows that many courses are not part of coherent programs, but are individual offerings whose content has little conceptual relationship to other courses. These institutions could very well serve student and group interests better, and strengthen their programs, by limiting the courses acceptable under diversity requirements and encouraging common conceptual frameworks across courses. Moreover, many institutions may need to make difficult choices to limit the expansion of ethnic studies programs if they do not have the resources to support such programs to reasonable levels of size and strength. Choices regarding ethnic studies may also depend upon the ethnic makeup of the campus and the institution's community of support. In the case of both multicultural and ethnic studies courses, institutions which now seek to raise enrollment in these courses by making them part of distribution requirements might consider deemphasizing enrolling large numbers of students in single courses through distribution requirements and put more emphasis on enrolling fewer students in concentrated programs such as certificates, minors, or majors.

A second model for change is to directly teach the conflicts that arise in the study of multiculturalism or among ethnic groups. This model has its origins in the concerns of some scholars about the divisive arguments over the canon and the related public debate in the late 1980s and early 1990s. In response to the consternation and polarization the debate has caused among his colleagues, Gerald Graff (1992) argues that the best solution to the conflicts over culture is to teach the conflicts themselves and to use them as an organizing principle to clarify and focus the curriculum. He believes that many academics who are skeptical about multiculturalism, feminism, and other new subjects would still agree that the questions and challenges posed by these new subjects deserve to be raised.

Graff emphasizes that the anger so prevalent in the campus debates over multiculturalism can be turned into positive debate. The focus for the curriculum can come from such lively topics and conflicts. Moreover, teaching about such conflicts would address the real problem: students don't understand the current debate. For many students, Graff says, the problem is how to deal with books in general, not which books should be in the canon. Teaching the conflicts would clarify the various positions in ways students can understand.

However, Graff acknowledges that building an intellectual community around conflict on college campuses is not likely to happen without programmatic effort. Part of this effort is developing more coherent and collaborative approaches. Graff suggests:

- The conflicts can be presented in jointly taught introductory courses.
- Faculty can co-teach courses, exchange courses, or have courses meet together periodically.
- Campus symposia or conferences can also be used to teach the conflicts.

A third model for change—and the one that appears to hold the most promise for utilizing the best of multiculturalism and ethnic studies within a single institution—is to teach and design curricula around integrative and comparative themes which cross the history and experience of many groups. This approach attempts to help students find meaning and understanding not only in the focused experience of their own group or one they have chosen to study, but in concepts such as group power, immigration, and access to jobs. Takaki (1993) points out that there are many studies that look at the history of one ethnic group. Students who want to study about a particular group—of which they may be a member—have a right to do so. However, a better approach is comparative and integrative, and Takaki uses it so that students can ask questions like, "How have the experiences of racial minorities such as African Americans been similar to and different from those of ethnic groups such as Irish Americans?"

This comparative and integrative approach offers many possibilities for individual courses, but also can serve as the organizing principal for departments or for a university-wide approach to melding multiculturalism and ethnic studies.

The important—and potentially controversial element—in this integrative and comparative approach is the precise nature of the common perspective, theme, or question that links the course together. For example, Takaki uses the framework of the international movement of labor to link the experience of various groups in America in relation to exploitation, racism, and discrimination. In a review of Takaki's *A Different Mirror: A History of Multicultural America*, Spring (1993) raises a number of questions about this approach:

- Will comparative and integrative history and education build cultural and racial tolerance or will it increase tensions?
- Should cross-cutting multiculturalism focus on the separate cultures comprising the United States or on how these cultures intersect to create an American culture?
- Is a comparative and integrative multicultural history and education primarily concerned with neglected and dominated groups in American society? Or is it about the interaction of all groups in American society?

Spring suggests an alternative concept for studying across groups, arguing that the most effective multicultural history is one written from the perspective of the cultural change resulting from the interactions of the cultures. He cites Takaki's discussion of Native Americans to show that even dominated groups influence one another.

Adam Meyer (1989–90) makes a case for a thematic approach across groups in regards to the study of literature. He maintains that using the simplistic, dualistic categories of "dominant" and "subordinate" to describe the relationship between ethnic groups is limiting. What is needed is an approach that captures the complexities of cross-ethnic relationships in the American ethnic experience.

One possible set of concepts around which to design such an integrative and comparative course is the approach to intergroup relations discussed in chapter 2. Such a course might begin with discussion and examples of ethnicity, race, and social class through the processes of acculturation and assimilation. Themes like social mobility, the role of unions in societal integration, and suburban migration could be explored. Furthermore, case studies from both the United States and other societies could be used to illustrate the economic, political, and social aspects of intergroup relations.

A fourth model for change is to establish an ethnic studies department or center, but one in which the focus is not on individual ethnic groups but on a holistic approach to ethnic studies. The center or program may take a comparative approach or include a collection of programs in various ethnic-group studies. It could also offer a degree in holistic ethnic studies while also offering programs on specific ethnic groups (Hu-DeHart, 1993).

International studies models may also prove helpful in teaching students about diversity while simultaneously strengthening their understanding of group—particularly their own group—values and participation in society. Early multicultural efforts included international studies. However, in the 1960s, likely influenced by the United States intervention in Southeast Asia and their opposition to the role that some scholars played in studying Third World societies on behalf of the U.S. government, some faculty most sympathetic to diversity identified area-study programs with neocolonialism. Moreover, some advocates of ethnic studies came to distrust persons other than group members who showed interest in a group and its region of origin. However, given that a sizeable portion of the diversity in American higher education is found in the children of immigrants, the reintroduction of international studies can be very useful. Moreover, there are particular issues and groups that can not be understood without bringing international connections up front. For example, the experience of many Hispanics in the United States can not be separated from an understanding of the migration to and from Central and South America and the conditions in those areas, both historical and contemporary.

Finally, for some advocates of multiculturalism and ethnic studies, the models for change are not conceptual but practical. They offer specific suggestions as to how institutions and faculty can better teach about differences. For example, for some who believe that multicultural education is on the ascendancy, the issue is no longer what students should learn about diverse cultures, but what strategies institutions should pursue. Examining differences and multiple cultural legacies in the classroom is the best way to deal with their complexities. The process is not easy, however. Gaff (1992) suggests these guidelines:

- Faculty must reach some kind of consensus on the definition of multiculturalism. A curriculum must be built with some agreement.
- The success of a program for the study of diversity in part reflects the institution's commitment to multiculturalism and diversity. Ultimately, however, success has to do more with faculty autonomy and workload.
- Students' educational goals should be clarified. Are students going to be learning about diversity because every educated person should know about

it? Because the knowledge will help them function in the global economy? Some other reason?

- Those promoting the study of multiculturalism will have to respond to critics who feel students don't know enough about American history and culture and thus need to spend more time in discipline-based courses.
- Should there be specific criteria for establishing an acceptable list of courses? A problem with having no specific criteria is that often many specialized courses, designed for majors in area studies, anthropology, or similar disciplines fall into an acceptable category of "non-Western cultures" but do not deal with issues important to general education and diversity.
- Faculty issues will include qualifications and preparation to teach (can non-group members teach about a group?) and faculty development.

Extracurricular Support for Diversity

Academic programs are an important aspect of promoting diversity and nurturing the values, culture, and participation of ethnic groups in higher education. In the preceding section we offered a number of strategies for strengthening these efforts, primarily by providing overarching frameworks that might help faculty organize instruction for addressing intergroup relations.

However, the higher education experience is much more than what goes on in the classroom. Moffett (1989) describes the complexity and depth of this experience in *Coming of Age in New Jersey*. Based on years of ethnographic study, he details how students construct lives outside and away from the faculty, their courses, and the formal curriculum. The early multicultural education efforts in the 1940s and 1950s recognized that lessons about diversity, ethnicity, and intergroup relations came as much from campus organizations and dormitories, and participation in student government, clubs, and other activities as they did from readings and seminars. Therefore, achieving goals of diversity and group recognition must also focus on the extracurricular aspects of campus life and build them into an overall campus strategy.

Among the issues that such a strategy must take into account are the following:

- The degree of support the institution should provide to ethnic-based student centers and organizations; these centers and activities may be connected to ethnic studies programs
- What policies to develop regarding the staffing of student organizations, coverage by the student press, the content of campus radio stations, and the nature of speakers and entertainment groups invited to campus

- The prevention and resolution of conflicts that arise over allocation of space to various groups or the appropriation of funds to various student groups by student governments
- Enforcement of nondiscrimination by campus organizations such as fraternities and sororities
- What approach to take to voluntary group segregation in housing arrangements, affiliation with particular activities (clubs, music groups, publications), and the informal use of particular areas of campus facilities

Cheatham (1991) offers an explanation for why organizations or activities may become identified with certain ethnic groups, even on campuses where multiculturalism is part of the curriculum. He argues that the unique sociocultural and psychosocial experiences of ethnic minority students have not been appreciated and therefore not incorporated into collegiate programming for these students. Ethnic minority students would be better served when their distinctive experiences have been identified and intentionally incorporated into campus life. To achieve this, those staff and faculty who would be helpful to ethnic minority students must increase their knowledge and appreciation of students' sociocultural and sociohistorical legacies.

In particular, Cheatham says, African American students have come in increasing numbers to predominately white higher education institutions where they have encountered many barriers to full participation in campus life that they do not encounter at historically black colleges. For example, faculty may ignore them or call on them less often in class.

Student development theory suggests that during the college experience there can be an intentional intervention to help develop a basic sense of personal identity. Developing competence, managing emotions, achieving autonomy, and clarifying purpose are among the goals of such interventions. In designing these interventions, Higbee (1991) argues that the cultural specificity of the ethnic minority student must taken into account. He argues that different student groups have different developmental needs and different approaches are required to address different ethnic groups' socialization needs.

One type of extracurricular program that can aid in promoting diversity and strengthening the culture and participation of ethnic groups (and other underserved groups) are developmental education programs for underprepared learners. They are typically intended to promote pluralism by empowering underprepared, culturally diverse students to compete successfully without lowering standards. Developmental education programs focus on the process of learning as well as content. The most effective programs for promoting pluralism and improving retention are those said to incorporate counseling and student development. In addition, Higbee notes that quality programs are marked by thorough assessment, affective and cognitive development, challenge and support, involvement with many people, intrusive counseling and advising, high standards and expectations, and excellent teaching.

Student resident halls can be an important element in achieving diversity and supporting group culture and participation. It is in these living units that many students are first brought together to live with or in close proximity to students who differ from themselves in ethnicity, culture, and social class. Moffett (1989) demonstrates how these living sites—where students spend so much time and interact so intensely with so many people—are the incubators of student culture. At the same time, they house a culture far removed from faculty, staff, and administrators. Student housing must also deal with pressures to preserve group culture and identity through specially designated formal living arrangements or informal groupings and for diversity to be engendered through other living arrangements or student life-sponsored activities. The staff who live in the halls—many of them students themselves—are a key to developing campus diversity, and training is central to their preparation to achieve the diversity goals (VanBebber, 1991).

A critical issue in the development of institutional policy and in related preparation of staff is how to understand and respect the need for single group activities, housing arrangements, and centers while also signalling to the campus community as a whole the need for support for intergroup communication and dialogue.

Campus Climate and Culture

Simultaneously preparing all students for diversity and ensuring that all ethnic groups are affirmed includes both the formal academic components and the extracurricular activities and programs discussed above. However, also vital to achieving these goals is the recognition that the institution's climate and culture—particularly its beliefs, values, and attitudes about intergroup relations—will be a crucial element in achieving these goals.

At present, the cultures of college and university campuses are faced with many challenges. Among these is the tension between those who support the right of individuals to speak out versus the obligations of the institution to protect against behavior offensive to groups. At times the issue revolves around how best to deal with persons who express strong, racist views that offend others on campus while also protecting freedom of speech. A recent incident in New Jersey illustrates the difficulty in shaping a climate and culture in light of such events.

A student-sponsored speech at Kean College in New Jersey in November 1993 in which a Nation of Islam minister attacked whites, Jews, and homosexuals created controversy at a school which is trying to achieve multicultural scholarship and racial diversity. Kean has about 12,000 students, 14 percent African American and 14 percent Hispanic. The president is a Hispanic woman and of the top five administrators below her, two are African American and two are Hispanic. Jewish students make up about 1 percent of the student body; 130 of the 650 faculty are Jewish.

The conflict centered on the view by some faculty that the administration did not react quickly enough to condemn the speaker's remarks. Criticism of the administration came from the New Jersey chancellor for higher education and from the president of the Jewish Faculty and Staff Association. The college president condemned the content of the speech but defended the speaker's right to voice his opinions. Criticism moved beyond the speech to accusing the college's multicultural efforts as being responsible for anti-Semitism and accusing African American faculty for purportedly holding to ideas based on race and racism. African American faculty rejected the criticism and spoke of discrimination against black faculty by a white power structure (Nordheimer, 1993).

Given the deep-seated intergroup conflicts in society and the tension in higher education between protecting group rights and ensuring academic freedom, higher education institutions will continue to be faced with situations such as the one at Kean. These conflicts can best be met with clearly articulated leadership by administration and faculty for a climate of campus diversity, and demonstrated support for building a culture that values both multiculturalism and group studies in whatever form appropriate to that institution.

Given the political and social climate we described emerging in the mid-1990s, higher education faculty and administrators may be most effective in conveying their support for both multiculturalism and group studies when they do so through broader support for social justice. Students, other educators, and persons from the many groups that vie in the multicultural and ethnic studies conflicts should hear a clear and consistent message that supports democratic values and social justice beyond the specifics of immediate intergroup relations issues on campus.

Conclusion

In conclusion, we return to the question: How do colleges and universities best prepare students for common citizenship in a diverse, democratic state while also nurturing group cultures, values, and institutional participation? In this chapter we began by noting that ethnic studies and multiculturalism, while often supportive of the same goals, are not always mutually supportive. Institutions may have to make difficult choices about where they invest fiscal, human, and political resources. We also noted that despite the widespread discussion—and the conservative cries of alarm—ethnic studies and multiculturalism are far from universal, playing little, if any, role in the day-to-day life of millions of students.

Institutions which set out to develop programs to address the question asked above face a number of constraints, including difficulties associated with institutional change, conflicts between ethnic studies and multicultural initiatives, and conservative opposition to the promotion of diversity.

At the same time, the demand for institutional action will increase as the underserved minority populations grow, high school students experience more diversity and expect more of the same in college, foundations and accrediting agencies advocate multicultural and ethnic studies efforts, and some in the public continue to believe that universities have a responsibility for assisting in intergroup relations.

We have reviewed various models for promoting these changes, including strengthening existing programs, teaching about intergroup conflicts, teaching particular themes across groups and over time, and using international or area-studies approaches.

Some institutions will have to choose between ethnic studies and multicultural approaches rather than implementing them in a complementary fashion. For most institutions, multicultural initiatives will be focused on first-year or other introductory courses in various disciplines. Faculty will broaden the curriculum of a course or teach a course in which diversity is addressed directly. We see particular promise in several approaches, including the direct teaching of the conflicts and the use of anthropological concepts in the design of curricula and materials.

Perhaps of equal or greater importance are out-of-class efforts to prepare students for diversity. These include resident hall programs; support for campus organizations that represent ethnic groups, women, gay and lesbian students, older students, and others who have not had equal access to higher education; and the demonstration of leadership and thoughtfulness about intergroup relations by administrators and faculty.

For some institutions, ethnic studies and the related support given to specific groups will be a more appropriate approach. Institutions with historically large enrollments of particular ethnic groups, those with close ties to ethnic communities, and some with already well developed ethnic studies programs can take this approach. For example, large, state-funded institutions in urban centers in California, the Southwest, and other areas of high minority enrollment are already heavily invested in ethnic studies programs and should remain so.

Those institutions which take this approach should be prepared to strengthen ties with ethnic communities and to fund programs to the degree that they can be competitive with others in the field and be on par with similar units in their institution. A most exciting area for future development in ethnic studies is in programs where a number of ethnic studies programs are combined in degree programs and those individual ethnic studies programs where ethnic studies are built around concepts such as the comparative study of ethnicity, social class, and gender. Such programs hold the promise of answering both parts of the questions that guided this chapter by preparing students for diversity and democracy while also affirming group culture and participation.

References

Adelman, H. (1991). Is Jewish studies ethnic studies? In J. E. Butler and J. C. Walter (Eds.), *Transforming the curriculum*, 169–85. Albany: State University of New York Press.

Aguirre, A., and Martinez, R. O. (1993). Chicanos in higher education: Issues and dilemmas for the 21st century. ASHE–ERIC Higher Education Report No. 3. Washington, D.C.: George Washington University, School of Education and Human Development.

Allport, G. W. (1954). *The nature of prejudice*. Reading, MA: Addison-Wesley.

Altbach, P. G. (1991). The racial dilemma in American higher education. In P. G. Altbach and K. Lomotey (Eds.), *The racial crisis in American higher education*, 3–18. Albany: State University of New York Press.

American Council on Education. (1989). *Eighth annual status report on minorities in higher education*. Washington, D.C: American Council of Education, Office of Minority Concerns.

Anderson, J. (1988). *The education of blacks in the South, 1860–1935*. Chapel Hill: University of North Carolina Press.

Anyon, J. (1979). Ideology and United States history textbooks. *Harvard Educational Review* 49(3): 361–86.

Asante, M. (1991). The Afrocentric idea in education. *Journal of Negro Education* 60(2): 170–80.

Astin, A. (1985). *Minorities in American higher education*. San Francisco: Jossey-Bass.

Aufderheide, P. (Ed.). (1992). *Beyond PC: Towards a politics of understanding*. Saint Paul, MN: Graywolf.

Auletta, G., and Jones, T. (1990). Reconstituting the inner circle. *American Behavioral Scientist* 34(2): 137–52.

Banks, J. A. (1993). The culture wars, race, and education. *Phi Kappa Phi Journal* 73(4): 39–41.

Barth, F. (1969). *Ethnic groups and boundaries*. The Little, Brown series in anthropology. Boston: Little, Brown.

Bayor, R. H. (1993, November). Historical encounters: Intergroup relations in a "nation of nations." *The Annals* 530:14–27.

Beckwith, F., and Bauman, M. (Eds.). (1993). *Are you politically correct?* Buffalo, NY: Prometheus.

Bennett, W. J. (1994, 4 December). Immigration: Making Americans. *Washinton Post*, C7.

Berman, P. (1992). *Debating P.C.* New York: Laurel.

Bernstein, A., and Cock, J. (1994, 15 June). A troubling picture of gender equity. *Chronicle of Higher Education*, B1–B3.

Bernstein, R. (1994). *Dictatorship of virtue: Multiculturalism and the battle for America's future*. New York: Alfred A. Knopf.

Berry, M. F., and Blassingame, J. W. (1982). *Long memory: The black experience in America*. New York: Oxford University Press.

Bourdieu, P. (1973). Cultural reproduction and social reproduction. In R. Brown (Ed.), *Knowledge, education, and cultural change*, 71–112. London: Tavistock.

Bowles, F., and DeCosta, F. (1971). *Between two worlds: A profile of Negro higher education*. New York: McGraw-Hill.

Bowser, B., Auletta, G., and Jones, T. (1993). *Confronting diversity issues on campus*. Newbury Park, CA: Sage.

Broccoli, A. (1977). *Antonio Gramsci y la educacion como hegemonia*. Mexico City: Editorial Nueva Imagen.

Brownstein, R. (1994, 8 August). Nation seeking common standards for social policies. *Los Angeles Times*, A5.

Brubacher, J., and Rudy, W. (1976). *Higher education in transition*. 3rd ed. New York: Harper and Row.

Buckley, W. F. (1994, 12 November). Yes, immigration law reform is long overdue. *Dominion Post*, B3.

Butler, J. E., and Schmitz, B. (1992, January/February). Ethnic studies, women's studies, and multiculturalism. *Change* 24:37–41.

Butler, J. E., and Walter, J. C. (1991). Praxis and the prospect of curriculum transformation. In J. E. Butler and J. C. Walter (Eds.), *Transforming the curriculum*, 325–30. Albany: State University of New York Press.

California State University. (1992). *Statistical Abstract*. Long Beach, CA: California State University.

Campbell, L. (1995, 15 March). Yale to return Lee Bass' gift: $20 million was for program killed by politics. *Fort Worth Star-Telegram*, 1.

Carmona, J. (1994, 30 March). Anti–gay initiatives cause anxiety on campuses. *Chronicle of Higher Education*, A32.

Carnoy, M. (1976). *Education and cultural imperialism*. New York: D. McKay Co.

———. (1992). Education and the state: From Adam Smith to perestroika. In R. F. Arnove, P. G. Altbach, and G. P. Kelly (Eds.), *Emergent Issues in Education*, 143–162. Albany: State University of New York Press.

Chandler, J. (1993, 16 December). One for the college history books. *Los Angeles Times*, B4–B5.

Cheatham, H. (1991). Identity development in a pluralistic society. In H. Cheatham (Ed.), *Cultural pluralism on campus*, 23–38. N.p.: American College Personnel Association.

Christy, R., and Williamson, L. (Eds.). (1992). *A century of service: Land–grant colleges and universities, 1890–1990*. New Brunswick, NJ: Transaction.

Clark Hine, D. (1990). Black studies: An overview. In R. L. Harris, D. Clark Hine, and N. McKay (Eds.), *Black studies in the United States*, 15–25. New York: Ford Foundation.

———. (1992). The black studies movement: Afrocentric–traditionalist–feminist paradigms for the next stage. *Black Scholar* 22(3): 11–19.

Cohen, Y. (1971). The shaping of men's minds: Adaptations to the imperatives of culture. In M. Wax, Stanley Diamond and Fred O. Gearing (Eds.), *Anthropological perspectives in education*. New York: Basic.

———. (1975). The state system, schooling, and cognitive and motivational patterns. In N. K. Shimahara and A. Scrupski (Eds.), *Social forces and schooling: An anthropological and sociological perspective*, 103–140. New York: David McKay.

Cole, J. B. (1991). Black studies in liberal arts education. In J. E. Butler and J. C. Walter (Eds.), *Transforming the curriculum*, 131–47. Albany: State University of New York Press.

Coleman, M. (1993). *American Indian children at school, 1850–1930*. Jackson: University Press of Mississippi.

Cook, L. (1947). Intergroup education. *Review of Educational Research* 17(4): 266–78.

————. (Ed.). (1950). *College programs in intergroup relations: A report by twenty–four colleges participating in the College Study of Intergroup Relations, 1945–49.* Washington, D.C.: American Council on Education.

Coughlin, E. K. (1992, 29 January). Scholars confront fundamental question: Which vision of America should prevail? *Chronicle of Higher Education,* A8, A11.

————. (1993, 24 March). Sociologists examine the complexities of racial and ethnic identity in America. *Chronicle of Higher Education,* A7–A8.

Daniels, R. (1988). *Asian America: Chinese and Japanese in the United States since 1850.* Seattle: University of Washington Press.

de los Santos, A., and Rigual, A. (1994). Progress of Hispanics in American higher education. In M. J. Justiz, R. Wilson, and L. G. Bjork (Eds.), *Minorities in higher education,* 173–94. Washington, D.C: American Council on Education, Oryx Press.

Dei, G. J. S. (1994, March). Afrocentricity: A cornerstone of pedagogy. *Anthropology and Education Quarterly.* 25(1): 3–28.

DeJong, D. (1993). *Promises of the past: A history of Indian education in the United States.* Golden, CO: North American.

DelFattore, J. (1992). *What Johnny shouldn't read.* New Haven: Yale University Press.

DePalma, A. (1992, 18 October). Massachusetts campus is torn by racial strife. *New York Times,* 8.

DeWitt, K. (1994, 15 August). Wave of suburban growth is being fed by minorities. *New York Times,* A1, A12.

————. (1994, 30 January). Smithsonian scales back exhibit of plane in atomic bomb attack. *New York Times,* A1.

Douglas, G. (1992). *Education without impact: How our universities fail the young.* New York: Birch Lane.

Dziech, B. W. (1995, 13 January). Coping with the alienation of white male students. *Chronicle of Higher Education,* B2.

Elson, R. (1964). *Guardians of tradition: American schoolbooks of the nineteenth century.* Lincoln: University of Nebraska Press.

Feagin, J. R. (1989). *Racial and ethnic relations.* Englewood Cliffs, NJ: Prentice Hall.

Ferrin, R. (1971). *A decade of change in free–access higher education.* New York: College Entrance Examination Board.

Fitzgerald, F. (1980). *America revised: History schoolbooks in the twentieth century.* New York: Vintage.

Foster, P. (1977, June/October). Education and social differentiation in less developed countries. *Comparative Education Review* 21(2,3): 211–29.

Frammolino, R. (1994, 6 March). Not all embracing multiculturalism. *Los Angeles Times*, 6B.

Fuchs, L. H. (1993,November). An agenda for tomorrow: Immigration policy and ethnic policies. *The Annals* 530:171–86.

Gaff, J. (1992, January/February). Beyond politics: The educational issues inherent in multicultural education. *Change*, 31–35.

Gates, H. L. (1992). African American studies in the 21st century. *Black Scholar* 22(3): 3–9.

Getman, J. (1992). *In the company of scholars: The struggle for the soul of higher education.* Austin: University of Texas Press.

Gilroy, P. (1994). *The black Atlantic: Modernity and double consciousness.* Chicago: Chicago University Press.

Glazer, N. (1977). Public education and American pluralism. In J. Coleman (Ed.), *Parents, teachers, and children: Prospects for choice in American education,* 85–109. San Francisco: Institute for Contempory Studies.

———. (1993, November). Is assimilation dead? *The Annals* 530:122–36.

Goldstein, B. (1994). Cultural diversity and curricular coherence. In D. Halpern (Ed.), *Changing college classrooms,* 109–27. San Francisco: Jossey–Bass.

Gordon, E. W., and Bhattacharyya, M. (1992). Human diversity, cultural hegemony, and the integrity of the academic canon. *Journal of Negro Education* 61(3): 405–18.

Graff, G. (1992). *Beyond the culture wars.* New York: W. W. Norton.

Greeley, A. M. (1969). *From backwater to mainstream: A profile of Catholic higher education.* New York: McGraw–Hill.

Greenhouse, L. (1994, 1 November). Justices agree to consider if university should finance a student religious magazine. *New York Times,* A13.

Hall, P. A. (1991). Beyond Afrocentrism: Alternatives for African American studies. *Western Journal of Black Studies* 15(4): 207–12.

Harbison, F. H. (1973). *Human resources as the wealth of nations.* New York: Oxford University Press.

Harris, R. L. (1990). The intellectual and institutional development of Africana studies. In R. L. Harris, D. Clark Hine, and N. McKay (Eds.), *Black studies in the United States,* 7–14. New York: Ford Foundation.

Hayes–Bautista, D. (1992, 28 October). Academe can take the lead in binding together the residents of a multicultural society. *Chronicle of Higher Education*, B1–B2.

Heath, C., and Guyette, S. (1984). *Issues for the future of American Indian studies*. Los Angeles: UCLA, American Indian Studies Center.

Hein, J. (1993, November). Rights, resources, and membership: Civil rights models in France and the United States. *The Annals* 530:97–108.

Henry, W. A. (1993, Fall). The politics of separation. *Time* (special issue), 73–75.

Higbee, J. (1991). The role of developmental education in promoting pluralism. In H. Cheatham and Associates, *Cultural pluralism on campus*, 73–87. N.p.: American College Personnel Association.

Hraba, J. (1979). *American ethnicity*. Itasca, IL: F. E. Peacock.

Hu–DeHart, E. (1993, September). The history, development, and future of ethnic studies. *Phi Delta Kappan* 75(1): 50–54.

Humphries, F. (1992). Land–grant institutions: Their struggle for survival and equality. In R. Christy and L. Williamson (Eds.), *A century of service: Land grant colleges and universities, 1890–1990*, 3–12. New Brunswick, NJ: Transaction.

Hunter, J. D. (1990). *Culture wars*. New York: Basic.

Jaschik, S. (1994, 2 November). Federal appeals court deals blow to minority scholarships. *Chronicle of Higher Education*, A52.

Jones, A. (1995, 6 January). Our stake in history standards. *Chronicle of Higher Education*, B1, B3.

Jones, E. P. (1991). The impact of economic, political, and social factors on recent overt black/white racial conflict in higher education in the United States. *Journal of Negro Education* 60(4):524–537.

Kennedy, R. (1993). Introduction: Blacks and the race question at Harvard. In W. Sollors, C. Titcomb, and T. Underwood (Eds.), *Blacks at Harvard: A documentary history of African American experience at Harvard and Radcliffe*, xvii–xxxiv. New York: New York University Press.

Kidwell, C. S. (1994). Higher education issues in Native American communities. In M. J. Justiz, R. Wilson, and L. G. Bjork (Eds.), *Minorities in higher education*, 239–57. Washington, D.C: American Council on Education, Oryx Press.

Kimball, R. (1990). *Tenured radicals: How politics has corrupted our higher education*. New York: Harper and Row.

La Belle, T., and White, P. (1979). Educational policy and intergroup relations: An international and comparative analysis. In J. N. Hawkins and T. J. La Belle (Eds.), *Education and Intergroup Relations*, 1–23. New York: Praeger.

La Belle, T., and Ward, C. R. (1994). Multiculturalism and Education: Diversity and Its Impact on Schools and Society. Albany: State University of New York Press.

Lawrence, J. (1994, 21 September). Americans are angrier, negative. *Los Angeles Times*, 1.

Leatherman, C. (1994, 2 March). All quiet on the Western Front—for now. *Chronicle of Higher Education*, A17.

———. (1994, 15 June). The minefield of diversity: How debate over expanding a multicultural requirement at the U. of Oregon got ugly. *Chronicle of Higher Education*, A15, A17.

Levine, A. (1991, September/October). The meaning of diversity. *Change*, 4–5.

Levine, A., and Cureton, J. (1992, January/February). The quiet revolution: Eleven facts about multiculturalism and the curriculum. *Change*, 25–29.

Low, V. (1982). *The unimpressible race: A century of educational struggle by the Chinese in San Francisco*. San Francisco: East/West.

Magner, D. (1991, 1 May). Push for diversity in traditional departments raises questions about the future of ethnic studies. *Chronicle of Higher Education*, A11–A13.

———. (1992, 11 March). Faculty members at Berkeley offer courses to satisfy controversial "diversity" requirement. *Chronicle of Higher Education*, A1, A16–A17.

Magner, D. K. (1993, 1 December). When whites teach black studies. *Chronicle of Higher Education*, A19–A20.

Majek, J. A. (1991). A critical asssessment of Bloom: The closing of an American mind? In J. E. Butler and J. C. Walter (Eds.), *Transforming the curriculum*, 26–37. Albany: State University of New York Press.

Manegold, C. S. (1995, 30 January). Appeals panel hears case against Citadel. *New York Times*, A1.

Mazumdar, S. (1991). Asian American studies and Asian studies: Rethinking roots. In S. Hume, H.–C. Kim, S. S. Fugita, and A. Ling (Eds.), *Asian Americans: Comparative and global perspectives*, 29–44. Pullman: Washington State University Press.

Mehan, H., Hubbard, L., and Villanueva, I. (1994, June). Forming academic identities: Accomodation without assimilation among involuntary minorities. *Anthropology and Education Quarterly* 25(2):91–117.

Merelman, R. M. (1994, February). Racial conflict and cultural politics in the United States. *Journal of Politics* 56(1): 1–20.

Meyer, A. (1989–90). The need for cross–ethnic studies: A manifesto (with antipasto). *MELUS* 16(4): 19–39.

Moffett, M. (1989). *Coming of age in New Jersey.* New Brunswick: Rutgers University Press.

Morin, R. (1995, 16 January). An army from academe tries to straighten out "The bell curve." *Washington Post,* A3.

Morley, J. (1995, 15 January). A P.C. guide to political correctness. *Washington Post,* C1, C4.

Murray, C., and Hernstein, R. J. (1994). *The bell curve.* New York: The Free Press.

National Conference of Christians and Jews. (1993). *Taking America's pulse: A summary report of the national conference survey on intergroup relations.* New York: National Conference of Christians and Jews.

National Council for Black Studies. (1994, Winter). New black studies units forged on black campuses; NCBS proving to be influential voice. *Voice of Black Studies Newsletter* 18(5).

Nelan, B. W. (1993, Fall). Not quite so welcome anymore. *Time* (special issue), 10–12.

Neusner, J. (1987, July/August). Ethnic studies. The coming crisis: The case of "Jewish studies." *Change* 19:8–10.

Nieto, S. (1993). Multiculturalism in higher education: Emerging literature. *Equity and Excellence in Higher Education* 26(3): 77–79.

Noble, K. B. (1994, 11 November). California's immigration measure faces rocky legal path. *New York Times,* A17.

Nordheimer, J. (1993, 29 December). College diatribe ignites furor on race and speech. *New York Times,* B1, B6.

Ogbu, J. (1978). *Minority education and caste: The American caste system in cross-cultural perspective.* New York: Academic.

——— (1987). Variability in minority school performance: A problem in search of an explanation. *Anthropology and Education Quarterly* 18(4): 312–34.

Okihiro, G. Y. (1991). African and Asian American studies: A comparative analysis and commentary. In S. Hume, H.-C. Kim, S. S. Fugita, and A. Ling (Eds.), *Asian Americans: Comparative and global perspectives,* 17–28. Pullman: Washington State University Press.

Oppelt, N. (1990). *The tribally controlled Indian colleges: The beginnings of self-determination in American Indian education.* Tsaile, AZ: Navajo Community College Press.

Orfield, G. (1989). Hispanics. In A. Levine, (Ed.), *Shaping higher education's future: Demographic realities and opportunities, 1990–2000.* San Francisco: Jossey-Bass.

Otuya, E. (1994). African Americans in higher education. *American Council on Education Research Brief Series* 5(3).

Park, R. E. (1950). *Race and culture.* Glencoe, IL: Free Press.

Perez-Pena, R. (1994, 30 December). A rights movement that emerges from the right. *New York Times*, A13.

Petersen, W. (1982). Concepts of ethnicity. In W. Petersen, M. Novak, and P. Gleason (Eds.), *Concepts of ethnicity*, 1–27. Cambridge: Belknap Press of Harvard University Press.

Pitsch, M. (1995, 13 September). Dole takes aim at "elitist" history standards. *Education Week*, 18, 20.

Plante, P., and Atwell, R. (1992). The opening of the American mind. *Educational Record* 73(1): 32–36.

Power, E. J. (1972). *Catholic higher education in America: A history.* New York: Appleton–Century–Crofts.

Public Broadcasting System. (1994). School colors. *Frontline.*

Ravitch, D. (1990). Multiculturalism: E pluribus plures. *The American Scholar* 59(3): 337–54.

Rosenbaum, D. E. (1994, 11 November). New majority's agenda: Substantial changes may be ahead. *New York Times*, A10.

San Juan, E. (1991). Multiculturalism vs. hegemony: Ethnic studies, Asian Americans, and U.S. racial politics. *Massachusetts Review* 32(3): 467–68.

Schermerhorn, R. A. (1970). *Comparative ethnic relations.* New York: Random House.

Schmidt, B. C. (1991, 6 May). Universities must defend free speech. *Wall Street Journal*, A–16.

Scott, J. W. (1991, November/December). The campaign against political correctness: What's really at stake? *Change*, 30–43.

Simon, R. J. (1993, November). Old minorities, new immigrants: Aspirations, hopes, and fears. *The Annals* 530:61–73.

Sleeter, C., and Grant, C. (1987). An analysis of multicultural education in the United States. *Harvard Education Review* 57(4): 421–44.

Smiley, M. (1952). *Intergroup education and the American college.* New York: Teachers College, Columbia University.

Sollors, W., Titcomb, C., and Underwood, T. (Eds.). (1993). *Blacks at Harvard: A documentary history of African American experience at Harvard and Radcliffe.* New York: New York University Press.

Spring, J. (1993). Multicultural history and education: Purpose and perspective. *Multicultural Education* 1(1): 17–19.

Spring, J. (1994). *The American school: 1642–1993.* 3rd ed. NewYork: McGraw–Hill.

Stein, W. (1992). *Tribally controlled colleges.* New York: Peter Lang.

Steinberg, J. (1994, 12 December). Is Western civilization truly worth $20 million? *New York Times*, B1, B2.

Steinberg, S. (1974). *The academic melting pot: Catholics and Jews in American higher education.* New York: McGraw–Hill.

Stolze, T. (1988). 1968 and democracy from below. *Against the Current*, n.s., 3(4): 9–13.

Strauss, J. H., and Pepion, K. (1992). Broken promises: An American Indian case study. *Thought and Action: The National Education Association Higher Education Journal.*

Szasz, M. (1974). *Education and the American Indian: The road to self-determination, 1928–1973.* Albuquerque: University of New Mexico Press.

Takaki, R. (1993, November). Multiculturalism: Battleground or meeting ground? *Annals of the American Academy of Political and Social Science* 530:109–21.

Teske, R. H. C., and Nelson, B. H. (1974). Acculturation and assimilation: A clarification. *American Ethnologist* 1:351–67.

Thomas, J. (1994, 11 November). U.S. history panel's history model looks beyond old Europe. *New York Times*, A1, A14.

Thompson, R. H. *Theories of ethnicity: A critical appraisal.* Contributions in Sociology No. 821989. New York: Greenwood.

Toth, C. (1990). *German–English bilingual schools in America: The Cincinatti tradition in historical context.* New York: Peter Lang.

U.S. Department of Justice. (1990). *Statistical yearbook.* Washington, D.C.: Department of Justice, Immigration and Naturalization Service.

VanBebber, L. (1991). Integrating diversity into traditional resident assistant courses. In H. Cheatham (Ed.), *Cultural pluralism on campus*, 89–116. N.p.: American College Personnel Association.

Washburn, D. E. *Ethnic studies.* Miami: Inquiry International.

Waters, M. C. (1990). *Ethnic options.* Berkeley and Los Angeles: University of California Press.

Wheeler, D. L. (1994, 7 September). Helping mixed–race people declare their heritage. *Chronicle of Higher Education*, A8.

Will, G. F. (1993, 31 May). Compassion on campus. *Newsweek*, 66.

William H. Donner Foundation. (1993). *Annual report*. New York: William H. Donner Foundation.

Williams, R. *The long revolution*. New York: Columbia University Press.

Wilson, R. (1994). The participation of African Americans in American higher education. In M. J. Justiz, R. Wilson, and L. G. Bjork (Eds.), *Minorities in higher education*, 195–209. Washington, D.C: American Council on Education, Oryx Press.

Winkler, K. J. (1991, 11 September). While concern over race relations has lessened among whites, sociologists say racism is taking new forms, not disappearing. *Chronicle of Higher Education*, A8–A11.

———. (1992, 25 November). Race, class, gender in American studies: "Mantra" or new conception of the field? *Chronicle of Higher Education*, A6–A7.

Wright, B. (1990, October). American Indian studies programs: Surviving the '80s, thriving in the '90s. *Journal of American Indian Education*, 17–24.

Young, C. (1984). The struggle and dream of black studies. *Journal of Negro Education* 53(3): 368–78.

Index

Other Books in This Series

Class, Race, and Gender in American Education
—Lois Weis (ed.)

Excellence and Equality: A Qualitatively Different Perspective on Gifted and Talented Education
—David M. Fetterman

Change and Effectiveness in Schools: A Cultural Perspective
—Gretchen B. Rossman, H. Dickson Corbett, and William A. Firestone

The Curriculum: Problems, Politics, and Possibilities
—Landon E. Beyer and Michael W. Apple (eds.)

The Character of American Higher Education and Intercollegiate Sport
—Donald Chu

Crisis in Teaching: Perspectives on Current Reforms
—Lois Weis, Philip G. Altbach, Gail P. Kelly, Hugh G. Petrie, and Sheila Slaughter (eds.)

The High Status Track: Studies of Elite Schools and Stratification
—Paul William Kingston and Lionel S. Lewis (eds.)

The Economics of American Universities: Management, Operations, and Fiscal Environment
—Stephen A. Hoenack and Eileen L. Collins (eds.)

The Higher Learning and High Technology: Dynamics of Higher Education and Policy Formation
—Sheila Slaughter

Dropouts from Schools: Issues, Dilemmas and Solutions
—Lois Weis, Eleanor Farrar, and Hugh G. Petrie (eds.)

153

Religious Fundamentalism and American Education: The Battle for the Public Schools

—Eugene F. Provenzo, Jr.

Going to School: The African-American Experience

—Kofi Lomotey (ed.)

Curriculum Differentiation: Interpretive Studies in U.S. Secondary Schools

—Reba Page and Linda Valli (eds.)

The Racial Crisis in American Higher Education

—Philip G. Altbach and Kofi Lomotey (eds.)

The Great Transformation in Higher Education, 1960–1980

—Clark Kerr

College in Black and White: African-American Students in Predominantly White and in Historically Black Public Universities

—Walter R. Allen, Edgar G. Epps, and Nesha Z. Haniff (eds.)

Textbooks in American Society: Politics, Policy, and Pedagogy

—Philip G. Altbach, Gail P. Kelly, High G. Petrie and Lois Weis (eds.)

Critical Perspectives on Early Childhood Education

—Lois Weis, Philip G. Altbach, Gail P. Kelly and High G. Petrie (eds.)

Black Resistance in High School: Forging a Separatist Culture

—R. Patrick Solomon

Emergent Issues in Education: Comparative Perspectives

—Robert F. Arnove, Philip G. Altbach, and Gail P. Kelly (eds.)

Creating Community on College Campuses

—Irving J. Sptizberg and Virginia V. Thorndike

Teacher Education Policy: Narratives, Stories, and Cases

—Hendrick D. Gideonse (ed.)

Beyond Silenced Voices: Class, Race, and Gender in United States Schools

—Lois Weis and Michelle Fine (eds.)

Troubled Times for American Higher Education: The 1990s and Beyond

—Clark Kerr

The Cold War and Academic Governance: The Lattimore Case at Johns Hopkins
—Lionel S. Lewis

Multiculturalism and Education: Diversity and its Impact on Schools and Society
—Thomas J. La Belle and Christopher R. Ward

The Contradictory College: The Conflicting Origins, Impacts, and Futures of the Community College
—Kevin J. Dougherty

Race and Educational Reform in the American Metropolis: A Study of School Decentralization
—Dan A. Lewis and Kathryn Nakagawa

Professionalization, Partnership, and Power: Building Professional Development Schools
—Hugh G. Petrie (ed.)

Promotion and Tenure: Community and Socialization in Academe
—William G. Tierney and Estela Mara Bensimon